FISHING SENSE

FISHING
SENSE

PHILIP WEIGALL

EXISLE
PUBLISHING

First published 2011

Exisle Publishing Limited
'Moonrising', Narone Creek Road, Wollombi, NSW 2325, Australia
P.O. Box 60–490, Titirangi, Auckland 0642, New Zealand
www.exislepublishing.com

National Library of Australia Cataloguing-in-Publication Data:

    Weigall, Philip.

    Fishing sense / Philip Weigall.

    ISBN 9781921497926 (hbk.)

    Fly fishing—Handbooks, manuals, etc.

    799.124

Designed by saso content & design pty ltd
Typeset in Adobe Caslon 11/16 by 1000 Monkeys Typesetting Services
Printed in China through Colorcraft Limited, Hong Kong

10 9 8 7 6 5 4 3 2 1

To Dad

CONTENTS

INTRODUCTION

NOT LONG AGO I was on the Motueka River in the north of New Zealand's South Island. At the beginning of that April day, my friend Felix and I had enjoyed modest success drifting nymph patterns deep in the faster runs. However, as the hours passed the early chill faded. We decided it was time to stop nymph fishing and drive upriver, searching for the dimples of trout rising to mayfly in the long flat pools by the roadside. After a couple of kilometres we found such a pool. Even from up on the road we could see at least a dozen trout swirling and sipping away. Unfortunately though, the pool was already taken. As we watched, a spin fisher appeared from beneath a poplar tree, threw his lure right across the densest concentration of fish and urgently cranked it back. We should have kept driving and found some fish of our own, but the sight of so many trout feeding so perfectly exerted a primal pull, and we watched for several minutes as the spin fisher reeled cast after harmless cast through the rises.

As certain as the flow of the river, the spinner's attempts were futile. I understood this fundamental fact because similar experiences, multiplied by hundreds, were what persuaded me to take up flyfishing so many years ago. Unless the stranger accidentally jagged a trout, I knew he wouldn't catch one. The fish were blind to anything but the small insects (probably mayfly) drifting down the current, and nothing but a fly would fool them.

I guess part of the reason Felix and I watched for as long as we did was the hope the spin fisher would give up and leave the pool to us. But when he made his third lure change, we grudgingly accepted this was an unlikely outcome, and so we drove off again to find a stretch of our own.

Fortunately, about a kilometre further upstream, we found an even better pool. We could glimpse the odd rise from the road through gaps in the yellowing willows, but it was only when we actually walked down to the river's edge and had a clear view of the 300-metre-long pool that we realised what we'd found. Never mind a dozen trout, there must have been hundreds rising along the length, and across a good deal of the breadth, of the pool. The cause of the frenzy was an endless stream of little blue-grey mayfly duns.

I strode to the river and tied on a size 14 Parachute Adams, which seemed a good approximation of the naturals. It turned out the fly pattern was right but the size wasn't. As often happens when trout are feeding on thousands of the one kind of bug, they form quite a clear image of what the next one should look like — and size 14 was one size too big. Fortunately I wasn't stubborn enough to persist once the fly was rejected a few times. A change to a size 16 was like changing from cabbage to crayfish, and I was soon catching, or at least fooling, one trout after the other.

With the right fly, presented properly, the fishing over the next few hours was about as good as it gets. The wind stayed away and the river drifted past, delivering an endless supply of duns which the fish patiently sucked down. The trout graded from small ones of a pound or so in the shallows almost at my feet, to a few under the autumn-tinted willows on the far side that looked several times heavier. I made some attempts to wade through the 3- to 4-pounders in the middle to cast to those monsters, but never quite made it. I suppose on some level I couldn't bring myself to spook fish I would normally crawl through blackberries for.

Once or twice between fish, I caught myself thinking about the spin fisher downstream. I wanted him to see this, to understand what was possible with a fly rod. I wasn't driven by a desire to show off: I've long ago learned that pride is a feeling to manage with great care when flyfishing — grateful satisfaction is a much safer option! It was more about knowing that, right there and then, there was no better way yet devised of fishing with a rod and I wanted even a stranger to have the opportunity to understand that.

In the event, the stranger never appeared. I imagine he eventually headed sadly home to tell anyone who listened about his encounter with dozens of uncatchable trout. But had he wandered down, and asked, 'What are you getting 'em on mate?' I would have firstly showed him the tiny fly. And then the flyfishing system I was using to deliver it.

Some people will try to tell you (if they haven't already) that flyfishing is an unnecessarily complicated way of catching fish — a sort of artificially created obstacle course for those who find other ways of fishing too easy. In fact, there is no other method of fishing that can mimic such a broad range of things fish feed on. On the Motueka that day with Felix, only flyfishing had any hope of working. Try bait fishing with a size 16 dun or casting a lure which resembles and behaves like a mayfly nymph. It can't be done.

It's part of flyfishing lore that the first European records of flyfishing (the better part of 1800 years old) describe Macedonians fishing for trout taking mayfly. It's a fair guess that the anglers of this era were interested primarily in acquiring food to eat, not sport. But because real mayflies couldn't be threaded onto a hook, they made pretend ones out of feathers. The results looked, and crucially *behaved*, like mayfly enough to fool the trout. Almost two millennia on, flyfishing is still the only way of fooling trout feeding on Motueka mayfly, and the most effective way of catching trout doing a lot of other things too.

This is probably a good time to address some of the imprecision that comes with flyfishing. One of my friends, who catches more fish than most, treats flyfishing very much as a sport. He approaches most challenges from the angle of physics or biology, and he considers quantities — the size and number of fish caught — as a pretty good measure of success. However another mate hardly 'thinks' at all when flyfishing, drifting instead into a hunting state when casting, looking for fish, even choosing flies. Everything occurs almost intuitively. He's just as successful as the first guy, although he's more inclined to choose less tangible elements, like scenery, outwitting a particularly difficult fish or finding a snug campsite, as the makings of a good day.

The way in which two different approaches can both be right is a thread that winds right through flyfishing. This is a point of frustration for some first coming to grips with the sport, who would rather there was a sort of prescriptive manual: this way is right, and that way is wrong. But ultimately, I like the fact that you can enjoy a cuppa with a whole group of experts after a long day on the water without any of them agreeing on, say, what the best fly was. I also like that, in almost any flyfishing situation you can imagine, there is probably a better way of catching a fish on a fly than has so far been devised.

It's said that more has been written about flyfishing than any other sport. I have absolutely no idea if this is true or not, but if it is, at least part of the reason is covered in the preceding paragraph. This is an activity that defies simple evaluation. Perhaps last Sunday you caught more fish after you changed to a Wee Creek Hopper. But was it the actual fly change that did the trick or a coincidental change in conditions — possibly an increase in real grasshoppers on the water, or a subtle upward shift in water temperature that spurred the trout's metabolism? Could it even be that you suddenly felt more confident when you plucked this earlier overlooked pattern from your box, and therefore fished more carefully and expectantly? Such variables cut across virtually every aspect of the sport and drive flyfishing analysts mad. Even those like me, who accept and indeed quite like the mismatch between accounting and flyfishing, are left scratching our chins from time to time and wondering.

After decades of flyfishing, I find that much of what I learn and discover only leads to more questions, in large part because, as hard as I try, I cannot actually get inside the head of a fish, or in this specific case, a trout. This isn't a negative by any means — one of the many appealing aspects of flyfishing is the fact that the puzzles it throws up are never entirely solved. You periodically put together enough pieces to feel satisfaction and the joy of success, but as for any sense of a whole jigsaw completed? Well, it doesn't quite happen.

So rather than making any claim to have 'nailed' flyfishing for trout in a single book, this one is simply about those things that have become, if you like, my flyfishing 'truths'. It's a collection of techniques, ideas, concepts, knowledge and equipment that, to the best of my objective observation, honestly seem to matter when it comes to catching trout.

A BIT ABOUT TROUT

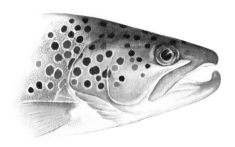

IT WAS BARELY the end of winter and Greg and I had ended up at Lake Echo in Tasmania's Central Highlands based on a mixture of hunch and logic. Earlier in the trip we'd concentrated on Arthurs Lake and Penstock Lagoon. 'Up top', these two lakes are the most sheltered, however during the gales that sweep the highlands, shelter is a relative term. The sky and the water were the same dull shade of grey, but for the streaks of white foam scarring the latter. It was hard to stand up and even harder to cast. We rarely saw a trout before we hooked it, and those few we caught were really just moments of random optimism, not clues to how or where we might catch more. Those occasional trout provided just enough impetus to persevere for the next hour or two.

There was some sense of satisfaction in catching anything at all under such trying conditions, and the highlands have a wild beauty that isn't diminished by bad weather. Nevertheless, when the gale was reinforced by drops of stinging rain, it was time to try somewhere else. We chose Lake Echo based on the high, sheltering ridges to its west (the same direction as the prevailing wind), and what might have been the glow of clearer skies right on the horizon, roughly in Echo's direction. There was also a recent positive report from a skilled and trusted friend.

The Echo decision was the right one. The sky was clearer, and the wind, while still roaring through the ridge-top forest above the lake, was reduced to occasional jabs at water level. Better still, a margin of freshly flooded grass and a liberal sprinkling of flotsam and jetsam, including various displaced bugs, indicated the lake was slowly rising. On any lake, rising water is likely to bring trout into the shallows to feast on flushed food; at Lake Echo such cause and effect is almost certain. This is partly because, as with so many Tasmanian storages, the lake has a close to perfect trout population profile. There are enough fish that any feeding opportunity is likely to be exploited as a result of competitive pressure, but there aren't so many fish that the overall food supply is insufficient and the trout become stunted or slabby.

Greg and I split up and began searching for fish. Initially we'd planned to head straight for the shallow grassy shores about a kilometre from where we'd parked the car, perfect for this floodwater feeding behaviour. A relatively small and gentle rise in level is a catastrophe on such shores if you're a burrowing beetle or browsing caterpillar, but a boon for foraging trout and stalking flyfishers.

However, it was soon apparent that even the steeper, rockier shores we had to walk past, guarded by the bleached sentinels of a long-drowned forest, were producing a steady supply of food too. With towering grey trunks all around — in the water and out — I began stalking carefully along the shore, looking for any sign of fish. I hoped to see a swirl or bow-wave, perhaps even a rise or the tip of a dorsal fin or tail. But the flooded edges dropped away at about 10 degrees, so even a trout moving along a bare metre or two offshore wouldn't necessarily disturb the surface. I needed to look carefully beneath the water, as well as on top of it.

Subsurface visibility wasn't ideal. Not only was the bottom a patchwork of sticks, rocks and clumps of newly drowned grass, but the shadows cast by the numerous trees also confused things. Additionally the sun came and went as wind-driven clouds raced by overhead. Successfully scanning beneath the water with polarised glasses is largely about distinguishing a fish that's designed not to be seen against its backdrop. The better lit that backdrop, and the more uniform it is, the less difficult it is to see the trout — and vice versa.

I was stepping carefully out onto a little rock island for a slightly better view into the water when I saw the first trout virtually at my feet. Bugger! I froze mid-stride, one foot on the shore, one on the rock, and waited for the fish to bolt in fright. But it didn't. To my amazement, its next action was to dart a foot to its left and almost between my waders to greedily grub some unseen morsel off the bottom. I was so close I could see the trout's eye turned down as it lined up the unfortunate bug it had located, then the vigorous chewing as it consumed it. Evidently, a combination of things — my upright shape lost among the dozens of other upright shapes of the tree skeletons, the trout's focus on feeding, and its sense of security cruising over a camouflaging bottom dotted with hiding places like logs and boulders — meant it didn't see or sense me.

I maintained my awkward statue stance just long enough for the fish to move a little further away. It darted for something a couple of metres ahead and I took the opportunity to bring my other foot onto the rock while removing my small black Woolly Bugger from the stripping guide. The Woolly wasn't designed to imitate anything in particular, but it has a proven record as a generalist fly under such circumstances: it's simply a buggy pattern that quivers and creeps with the slightest current or movement.

The trout moved off again, and I took my chance. Under normal circumstances it was still too close for a safe presentation (it was just over a rod length away) but I counted on the trout's preoccupied behaviour and the confusion of the dead trees around me to get away with it. It took a single flick to deliver the fly an arm's length to the left of the fish and slightly behind it. 'Never attack the fish with the fly' is good advice at moments like this. The trout started at the plop, not in fear but in an effort to detect where the noise came from, then in a moment it turned, just in time to see the Woolly settle to the bottom. It rushed over excitedly and chewed the fly aggressively, as if trying to disable it as much as eat it. I lifted the rod, confident the fish would be well hooked. It fled for deeper water even before the rod tip was upright and the game instantly changed from hooking to landing. I had a decent Lake Echo brown trout on the end, 3 pounds at least and approaching prime condition after weeks of bountiful rising water.

I was using 8-pound tippet, but I had to push it to the limit to keep the powerful fish away from the flooded bushes and snags that suddenly seemed to be everywhere. Yet keep it away I did, and eventually I was able to lead the fish to my landing net. As I knelt on the rock and gently pushed the hook out of its jaw scissors, I took a moment to contemplate what amazing creatures trout are, and all the things about them that worked for me — and potentially against me — in catching this one. Then I stood up, checked the tippet for abrasions (none surprisingly) and went looking for the next one.

While some people are obstinately uninterested in flyfishing, most can at least be persuaded that trout are interesting animals. Suppose you are a trout. Your field of vision is so wide that the only blind spot is a small area behind your head. You can use either eye independently to scan for food or danger then, if you want to grab a dragonfly scooting along a metre above the water, you can employ both eyes to precisely calibrate distance and snatch it from mid air. Meanwhile, your capacity to see in low light is extraordinary — even a cloudy, moonless night provides ample illumination to locate prey.

On those rare occasions when you can't see very well, there are other senses to fall back on. You don't have an externally obvious ear, but you do have an inner ear on each side of your head that is very good at picking up aquatic sounds. Coupled with a sensitive lateral line which lets you 'feel' vibrations, this means you have no trouble detecting a school of nervous minnows hidden in a muddy backwater, the plip of a beetle landing behind you, or the careless footfall of an angler 50 metres downstream.

As for sense of smell, it's so powerful as to be beyond a mere human's comprehension. Put it this way. Say you're living in a pure, wilderness river flowing at the rate of an Olympic swimming pool a minute, and a human steps into the edge of a pool 200 metres upstream. By the time the water that brushed their skin reaches you a few minutes later, it has been massively diluted, maybe to a few molecules per megalitre. Even so, you can smell the potential danger.

For a wild trout, just surviving to catchable size is miracle enough. Trout lay roughly 1000 eggs per kilogram of body weight, yet from all those potential offspring only two or three typically survive to adulthood. Everything from water beetles and dragonfly larvae to bigger trout want to eat trout fry and fingerlings, and of those aquatic creatures that don't actually eat them, many want to compete for food and space. Growing up in such a ruthless world, I guess it's no wonder the adult survivors display traits that we describe with words like 'cunning', 'discriminating' and 'wary'.

The most universal trout species are rainbow trout (*Oncorhynchus mykiss*) and brown trout (*Salmo trutta*), which exist in wild populations — endemic or introduced — on every continent except Antarctica. Although genetically quite distinct (rainbows are native to North America, browns to Eurasia), the two have a lot in common in terms of physiology and lifecycle. In fact, at times it can be difficult to tell them apart. When found in open-water environments or over light-coloured substrate, maidens (pre-mature fish) of both species can share a silvery fine-spotted appearance that's very similar.

There are some differences between rainbows and browns that are useful for flyfishers to be aware of. I'm generalising here, but I think of rainbows as the 'live fast, die young' species. They're often more energetic and less cautious feeders than browns, and this has several consequences of interest to flyfishers. For example, rainbows will utilise areas and food sources browns won't. Lake rainbows, for instance, can grow to respectable size and maintain good condition in deep, relatively sterile lakes that browns can struggle in. It seems their willingness to feed long and hard, if need be on very small food, stands them in good stead in such environments. (Large rainbows also have significantly finer gill rakers than large browns, meaning they can sift food too small for brown trout — a positive adaptation to food-poor habitat.) Rainbows have also established reputations as fish of the fastest sections of rivers, not because they can't utilise the slower stretches well (they can) but because they will feed in very swift, open currents if food availability warrants it — something browns do less.

The most obvious result of the more restrained behaviour of brown trout is that they are less easily caught. Where rainbows and browns co-exist, the former are usually caught several times more easily. In heavily fished waters, this catchability works against rainbows and in favour of browns. In a number of stocked lakes in western Victoria where I live, the rainbows are mostly all caught within a few months of release and so hardly ever attain a decent size, despite growing faster than browns. It's also probable that a rainbow's more reckless feeding behaviour works against it with other predators too. Enthusiastic open-water feeding is likely to make them more vulnerable to predators like pelicans and cormorants, while more cautious behaviour makes the browns harder for predators of all kinds to catch. In terms of potential size then, it's a bit of a case of the hare and the tortoise. Initially the rainbows grow faster, but the browns may patiently overtake their rainbow cousins simply by the trick of living longer.

Rainbows face another limit to their lifespan: the stress of spawning. To go back a step, most flyfishers are familiar with the spawning cycle, when both female browns and rainbows lay their eggs in suitable gravel redds (nests), to be fertilised by the milt of the males. Browns tend to run to spawn a bit earlier (late autumn/winter) than rainbows (winter/early spring). This is an extraordinary subject on its own, and spawning impacts directly and indirectly on flyfishing opportunities (more about this later in the book). However, in the context of browns versus rainbows, spawning is interesting in terms of how 'the cost' of it impacts the respective species. The rigours of spawning include a long period without much eating, diversion of energy to produce eggs and milt, and fighting over prime spawning sites, not to mention significant migration in many cases.

To put it simply, it seems rainbows pay a higher spawning 'price' than browns. Although spawning is not invariably lethal, as it is for their *Oncorhynchus* relatives, the Pacific salmons, it really knocks rainbows around, to the point that few live to do it twice. Certainly, rainbows do almost all their growing as maidens; i.e. before maturing. In fact post-spawning rainbows often struggle even to recover to their pre-spawning weight, let alone pass it. So significant is the spawning 'ceiling' to rainbow trout growth that in New Zealand's Rotorua district there is a program to selectively breed from late-maturing rainbows. The objective is to develop strains of fish that mature at three or four years of age, rather than two years, thus adding an extra year or two of growth before sexual maturity and spawning cuts in.

While rainbows tend to grow faster than browns and live shorter lives, both species are able to pretty much grow to match their environment, a trait that allows them to exploit a great range of waters. Trout can exist comfortably anywhere from the open ocean to the tiniest creeks, and they achieve this partly by not outgrowing the available resources. It's worthwhile to consider sea-run brown trout (trout which spend part of their life in rivers and part at sea) as an example. The progeny of a single pair of sea-runners is likely to include offspring that journey out to sea like their parents, but also some that remain in freshwater all their lives. In an area like the west coast of Tasmania, where many freshwater streams are quite infertile, this can mean that a given trout reaches no more than a handspan in length no matter how long it lives, while its sibling feeding in the fertile ocean grows to 20 pounds. Both trout will be healthy and well proportioned; they've simply grown to match the available food and space.

This relativity is something that every flyfisher should think about. A 12-inch trout in a rainforest creek may be an old survivor, a one-in-10,000 fish that's made it through several years when virtually every trout of the same year class has gone. In a way, such a trout is comparable to a trophy in a larger, more productive river. I'm not suggesting you should be as thrilled about catching the 12-incher as the 20-pounder — that would be hypocritical! However, it is worth remembering that big is a relative thing in the world of trout, and it would be a pity to overlook a remarkable capture just because the photo won't cause jaws to drop.

An interesting and related point is that the growth potential of both brown and rainbow trout is greatest in their first few years of life. As I touched on earlier, sexual maturity tends to be the growth ceiling for rainbows, and even those that live for another year or two grow very little compared to the exponential growth rates of the juveniles. Our studies at Millbrook Lakes, where I guide, typically show rainbow trout stocked at 50 grams growing to over 500 grams in less than six months — a tenfold increase. But the relative growth rate usually slows after that and tends to stop altogether well before a rainbow reaches the end of its life. While the browns grow more slowly and grow for longer, even they reach a plateau: although we've caught some very old browns at Millbrook — as old as twelve years — they tend to be no bigger than browns half that age.

Another useful species-survival mechanism employed by trout is a propensity to migrate — or not. Some trout are the ultimate homebodies, spending their entire lives in the vicinity of a single pool. These are (or can be) those trout you imagine you catch from the same spot in front of/behind that log/branch/rock year after year. True, sometimes it's just the spot being so good that guarantees a respectable but different trout on each visit. However, sometimes a distinguishing mark or scar proves that it is indeed the same fish, content to feed and maybe even spawn in the same few metres of stream.

At the other extreme are the wanderers, trout that seem to have some genetic predisposition to migrate to an unbelievable degree, even if their kin are reluctant to leave the same stretch of lakeshore or river. These are the giant trout you find in the inaccessible headwater lakes in Tasmania; fish that at some point must have pushed their way over little more than wet grass, despite their mission more likely ending in stranding and death than exclusive access to a competition-free lake. Other trout just seem to wander for the sake of it, although I can hear my fisheries biologist mates tut-tutting at such a simplistic explanation! My friend and noted guide Craig Simpson caught a tagged trout in a prime stream in the Murchison area of New Zealand that had been tagged in another, distant prime stream eighteen months earlier. Exactly why a trout would travel over 70 kilometres (the shortest distance by water between the release and recapture points) to abandon one very healthy stream for another is a mystery. What's more, the journey involved a mixture of downstream and upstream migration. And that's nothing compared to other trout which have been tracked not only travelling hundreds of kilometres but completely changing watersheds too.

One consequence of all this is how quickly trout can recolonise waters that have been decimated by local disasters. So long as there are trout left somewhere within reach, you can be sure that the wanderers will move back in as soon as conditions are suitable. And in a happy example of the balance of nature, because such trout initially have the lake or stream in question all to themselves, they grow quicker and spawn more successfully. Following natural disasters, I've seen rivers like the Macalister and Buckland in my home state of Victoria go from being totally devoid of fish of any kind to recovering trout stocks within three years so well that you wonder if you imagined the whole thing. Droughts, heatwaves, extreme floods and other events will always be depressing to flyfishers, but there is comfort in knowing that, given half a chance, trout are basically designed to come back.

FEEDING

PART OF THE reason trout have become such an iconic sportfish in both hemispheres is surely tied in with their feeding behaviour. Before I go any further, I need to remind me as much as you that trout are comparatively primitive predators. They can't reason like we can, they eat their own babies if they can catch them, and they can't analyse things well enough to avoid taking flies with obvious, protruding fish hooks.

Having established that trout aren't actually small people in fish suits, I hope you'll excuse a little anthropomorphic language when describing their feeding behaviour. Trout might be primitive but they're undoubtedly effective hunters, and understanding how they operate can be helpful when flyfishing for them.

I've come to think of feeding trout as Jekyll and Hyde characters. In one sense they can be aggressive, almost shark-like — an essential characteristic of any successful predator — but this aggression is mitigated by caution, because madly chasing down everything small enough to eat isn't always the most effective (or safest) feeding strategy.

An interesting generalisation can be made that a trout's feeding aggression and 'recklessness' increases with food abundance, physical comfort and the sense of security offered by features that help conceal it — like low light, broken or discoloured water and structure. Conversely, caution and timidity become more pronounced with a diminishing of any of the above.

Another issue that can be considered separately is opportunistic versus selective feeding behaviour. Back to the predator thing again and, superficially at least, opportunistic feeding (that is, eating anything encountered that falls within the parameters of prey) seems the smart way to go. Whether you're a lion, a falcon or a trout, you're only as successful as your last meal, so being fussy doesn't appear to make much sense. And indeed, in most trout waters most of the time, this logic is borne out. The stomach contents of a trout typically include several kinds of food. This is often a mix of small, 'boring' things like beetles, nymphs and various aquatic larvae, interrupted by the odd surprise like a large yabby, mouse or lizard, as if to emphasise the opportunistic predator thing.

So how is it that so much mythology about selective feeding and 'matching the hatch' has grown up around flyfishing for trout? The simple answer is that for a small but significant percentage of most trout's lives, selective feeding is, in fact, a biologically efficient strategy. Moreover, at such times trout feeding is often at its most spectacular, and matching the hatch is indeed essential to success.

The driver for selective feeding is when one type of prey becomes so abundant and easy to catch that it makes sense for the trout to focus their attention on it to the exclusion of all else. Suppose there's a plague of grasshoppers along a Snowy Mountains stream, or a mass migration of flying ants over a lake in the Tasmanian Central Highlands. Once abundance passes a certain point, trout quite sensibly dedicate themselves to that food source alone. Beats or lies are chosen on the basis of grasshopper or ant availability. Then the repetition of dozens of near-identical prey items drifting past rapidly develops a quite precise search image in the trout's brain. Very soon, often a matter of minutes after the quantity of the 'new' prey overwhelms everything else available, I imagine the trout put on a pair of proverbial blinkers. They don't merely refuse anything that's not an ant or a hopper, they effectively don't see it, such is their preoccupation with capitalising on the brief abundance.

At times like this, flyfishers are known to rail at the absurdity of a trout ignoring a big juicy minnow fly — or even a real minnow — in favour of a tiny ant. But let's face it: during the period (often only a short period) when the ants, mayfly or whatever are available, they represent a massive supply of helpless, easy-to-catch food. The trout can vacuum them up like whales sieving krill, and the energy profit is huge. Why leave the sure thing to dash off after a minnow that might escape?

Not for the only time, those trying to understand trout feeding behaviour must put aside what they as anglers 'want' (even subconsciously); thoughts such as 'Let the fish like the fly I have on now because I don't want to have to change it in the dark'; or 'The fish are breaking the surface so that means I can use my favourite, the dry fly', and so on. There is a logical, commonsense explanation behind everything a trout does, feeding included, but to appreciate that you must make the effort to understand how a trout thinks, not what *you* think or what you would like the trout to think.

So selective feeding requires the right choice of fly and we have to try to imagine what it is a trout is looking for. Again, this isn't always what is most apparent to us. Some very nice looking dry flies fail because the obvious bit to the angler — the bit above the water — is all but irrelevant to the trout, which of course views all dry flies from beneath. That brings me to the two fundamental characteristics that must be present in any successful fly for selective trout (or, I guess, in any fly for that matter): an acceptable appearance and acceptable behaviour.

When I was a kid, mudeyes (dragonfly larvae) were the best bait on my local streams, period. However, they were often desperately hard to find; it could take two hours to find enough for an hour's fishing. When I stumbled on a batch of plastic mudeyes at the local sports store, I thought I'd found the answer to the mudeye problem. The moulded copies were perfect replicas of the real thing, complete with bulging eyes, six legs with joints, and a segmented body. I spent all my pocket money on four of these wonders, assuming my days of crawling around for hours turning over rocks looking for the real insect were over.

The reality was a crushing disappointment. Using my spinning rod, with a couple of split shot for casting weight, I prospected all my favourite runs and pools for not a single trout. Only once, a year or so after I'd basically given up on the plastic mudeyes, did one actually work. In what must have been one of my earliest experiences of sight fishing, I spotted a huge trout feeding in a short plunge pool on a steep section of the upper Mitta Mitta River. Intuitively I knew it wouldn't fall for my Celta lure, so in desperation I changed to the mudeye. In hindsight, my cast was perfect, landing the imitation in a cascade just ahead of the trout. It must have had only a glimpse of the mudeye shape ahead of it in the fast, turbulent water before it snatched the fraud, and was hooked. That 4-pounder was the biggest trout I was to catch for years, and so I suppose all that pocket money was worth it in a way.

I may have barely grasped the point at the time, but I look back at the plastic mudeye and recognise it was about as realistic to the trout as a mannequin in a shop window is to us. The appearance was near perfect but its behaviour in the water was utterly wrong. The fake mudeye was effectively a statue in the water, its precise anatomical detail no compensation for its rigid, lifeless nature. The plastic mudeye only worked on that one big fish because there wasn't time for its wooden behaviour to be exposed.

Effective flies must at least suggest life, be that via the movement of soft materials, a certain way of sitting on or in the water, and so on. Today, the mudeye patterns I use are much cruder replicas of the real insect than those early plastic mudeyes — sometimes no more than roughly the same profile and with no detail at all — but they move like a real mudeye, or at least they can be made to move like a real mudeye, and the trout are usually fooled.

Selective trout seem to quickly establish a key feature or features of the abundant food type, which they then rely on to distinguish it from all the other distractions drifting around in the water. As many flyfishers before me have worked out, it seems these 'trigger' features are almost a shorthand way for the trout to pick the wheat from the chaff, so to speak. Instead of having to do, say, an elaborate leg count, the fish pick one or two obvious features and hone in on them. The interesting part for the angler is working out which features exactly *are* the key ones? Back to mudeyes, and trout targeting migrating mudeyes after dark look for a basic mudeye silhouette, and a 'dip ... pause and float ... dip' motion. Grasshopper feeders look for a body of roughly the right colour, floating but breaking the surface film like the hull of a tiny boat. And the trout like the dinner-bell plop as a grasshopper lands. My friend Peter Hayes tells me he can persuade dedicated hopper feeders to grab a hook with a couple of matchsticks glued to it — the 'fly' is straw-coloured, about the right size and it makes a satisfying plop.

Sometimes selective feeders will go one step beyond targeting a particular prey and dedicate themselves to a certain stage or state of that prey. Smelters (baitfish feeders) may focus on sick or injured baitfish whose colour change ability is disabled. For the angler, fooling such fish may require a fly that's actually a *different* colour to the healthy minnows. Meanwhile trout feeding on emerging insects like midge or mayfly will end up targeting the most vulnerable, easy-to-catch stage. The actual 'emerger', half undressed if you like, is one obvious choice — unable to swim, unable to fly, and anchored in the surface film by a partially shed shuck. This stage only lasts for a few seconds but flies which 'freeze' this point, like Klinkhammers and Possum Emergers, can be deadly when patterns suggesting the fully emerged adult (the most obvious stage to the angler) are ignored.

Of course, there are times when trout won't feed at all, selectively or otherwise. Fortunately, compared to many other species of fish these periods are rare. However, trout that have been scared by predators (cormorants, for example, can cause them to hide for hours) simply won't feed and are therefore uncatchable. Likewise, trout stressed by extreme water conditions such as low dissolved oxygen or heat (often but not always related) are too busy trying to survive to eat. It's time to find somewhere else to fish.

HIDING

TROUT ARE INCREDIBLY good at hiding. In terms of physiology, they have cells called chromatophores in their skin that are capable of quite chameleon-like feats. Chromatophores can very quickly lighten or darken the skin in response to changes in a trout's background. When transferring trout from shady hatchery ponds to cream-coloured fibreglass transport tanks, I've watched the fish lighten in a matter of minutes. In the wild, trout spending time over sandy substrate will soon become appropriately pale, while fish mere metres away over weed or bedrock are dark. The easiest trout to see are those that regularly move from one backdrop to another or those that are ill or blind. The chromatophores of injured or sick trout often fail to operate correctly, while blind fish perceive the world as black and invariably turn unnaturally dark themselves. Interestingly, trout that are blind in one eye usually turn uniformly dark through one hemisphere and retain normal colour through the other.

Over time, healthy trout can develop quite sophisticated changes in appearance beyond merely lighter or darker. They can literally change colour, with, say, trout from tannin-stained waters soon taking on a wonderful golden-brown hue, while sea-runners fresh from the open ocean are chrome silver. (Surprisingly, silver is an excellent form of camouflage in open, clear water: from above, silver fish appear almost translucent.) While browns, in their typically cryptic fashion, are the best overall at camouflage, rainbows can certainly melt away at times.

Besides changing their appearance, trout are very good at using things like structure, shadow, broken water and so on to aid concealment. I often marvel at how large trout seem to intuitively know their own dimensions and will find feeding lies around boulders that are at least their own length, thus successfully breaking up their outline. Meanwhile, smaller trout in the same stream will cheerfully hold near regular-size rocks and achieve the same effect.

Trout seem to appreciate the value of broken water too, and for good reason. I will never forget one fish on the Ahuriri River in the central South Island of New Zealand. The river was low by its usual boisterous standards and I'd just polaroided a 3-metre deep, silt-bottomed pool on an anabranch for no result. I'd felt sure that this refuge would hold a couple of big trout, but although the light was perfect under a midday summer sun and the water clear except for the faintest glacier-blue tinge, I couldn't see any sign of life. I stared until my eyes watered, crossed the river and stared again. Nothing.

Defeated, I started walking upstream in search of the next holding water. I paid no attention to the long, ankle-deep riffle above the pool until I saw rise right in the middle of it. I would have dismissed the rise as belonging to a tiddler if not for the loud 'clop' that went with it. Intrigued, I stopped and watched from a few metres downstream. It seemed I could see into the shallow water easily, and although the riffle's surface was indeed riffled, the substrate was made up of golf-ball-sized gravel and I was sure I would have spotted any half-decent trout lying over it. Then there was another solid rise, and with the aid of this exact visual cue, I imagined just for a moment I could make out the shape of a trout. It was more a subtle change of light than a distinct fish, as if what I glimpsed was made of glass. Then the mirage was gone again and I was looking at an empty riffle.

Bewildered, I knelt low and cast anyway to a point a metre or so above the rise: at least that had seemed genuine! My Shaving Brush dry drifted down the current, and right at the spot, a large head emerged from the water and inhaled the fly. I struck and the virtual trout became very real, rooster-tailing down and out of the riffle that barely covered it and into the previously vacant pool below. Here it bull-dogged away for ages, before surprisingly making a dash for an almost identical riffle below. Just as it made the shallows, I was able to apply enough side-strain to beach it. It took only moments to pull the Shaver free and guide the 4-pound brown trout back into the downstream riffle. At first it was quite easy to see as it hovered a few centimetres above the gravel and cast a shadow. But then it found a depression and settled right to the bottom, its fins and tail barely moving as it did the trout equivalent of catching its breath. Hard on the streambed like a flathead, and aided by the ripple overhead, the fish seemed to almost merge with the gravel. In clear water less than a handspan deep and lit by an overhead sun, a 2-foot trout I could have reached out to touch had all but vanished. I've never forgotten that fish, and every time I scan a lake flat or riverbed and think 'no trout', I remember that Ahuriri brown and mentally add the rider 'maybe'.

There are two problems with an angler overestimating their ability to see trout. The first, as per my Ahuriri experience (almost!), is walking right past catchable trout, not only scaring and missing that chance but often creating an unfortunate chain reaction of spooked fish. The second problem is that not seeing fish can cause people to think trout are not there, especially if not seeing is combined with not catching. Almost weekly I receive reports from anglers who are convinced that this lack of contact equates to the trout being absent. 'Nothing home I'm afraid, Phil,' they tell me sadly, citing evidence like, 'The water was really clear, but I didn't even spook any.' This leads to conclusions such as, at best, no trout being present in a given stretch of river or lakeshore, and at worst, trout gone from the water altogether.

Well, I don't know how to put this politely, but a human not seeing or catching trout means bugger all in terms of what's home or not beneath the water. If I needed any further convincing of this fundamental fact, several years ago a couple of fisheries scientists with all the right permits invited me on an electro-fishing trip to a small Victorian trout stream to check on the winter spawn run. Following a serious safety briefing (the electric charge involved could kill a horse, literally), we decked out in full-length waders and rubber gloves, and started wading up the 5-metre-wide mountain stream. One of my companions, Ian, carried a backpack charger which bristled with ominous warnings, while the other, Paul, carried a long-handled net ready to scoop up any shocked fish.

We came to the first significant pool, about the size of a living room. It was no more than calf deep, and although the July sun wasn't strong, it lit the ice-clear water of the pool sufficiently to determine that no trout were visible. Ian offered the compulsory warning, his backpack hummed, and then he discharged the current into the water via a device not unlike an oversized metal detector.

Electro-fishing works by making the muscles that face the electrical field contract, causing any fish inside the field to briefly spiral uncontrollably. As a bonus, this movement also displays their white bellies, making them extra visible. However, for reasons to do with the distance between the 'poles' of the creature being shocked, the current is much less dangerous to a trout than a human. It only takes a few seconds for the stunned fish to recover, so the guy on the net has to be quick.

Within an instant of Ian discharging the electro-fisher, a foot-long trout came wheeling out from the left bank. Paul jabbed his net under it with heron-like speed, and soon a confused brown was swimming in a large bucket on the bank, to await weighing and measuring before release. I was mildly impressed, partly because the system actually worked and partly because the trout came from a spot that looked too insignificant to conceal a fish.

The next pool was bigger, perhaps 10 metres long and half a metre deep, with a small log lying diagonally across its sandy bottom. Once again, a careful search of the pool before we stepped in showed no sign of a trout, but based on the previous pool, I was confident the electro-fisher would reveal a pounder or two hiding in there somewhere. Ian's backpack hummed again, he stuck the device in the water, and suddenly there were fish going everywhere. And they weren't pannies, but beauties — huge spawners of 2 to 3 kilograms, no doubt migrants from the large river downstream. Paul managed to scoop three into the bucket but at least that many escaped.

Never before or since have I witnessed a more definitive display of the ability of trout to be utterly invisible. This pool was clear, shallow, well lit and lacking in cover apart from one modest, half-buried log, and the banks weren't undercut by more than a few centimetres. We had approached the pool without spooking any fish, and three trained sets of eyes had failed to detect so much as a suspicious shape or movement. When Ian shocked the pool, it was as if the machine manufactured the fish, creating them out of thin air, or should that be thin water?

In the years since, I've recalled that day many times when fishing water that appears empty of trout. I have to remind myself that salmonids pretty much choose whether they want to be seen, so any angler who believes not spotting fish means they're not there is mistaken.

If I ever need the hiding trout lesson reinforced, it happens every time I'm involved with trout stocking. When stocking relatively low numbers of small fish, we forego the fibreglass trailer tanks and use plain old 44-gallon drums. The yearlings we transport are usually 15 to 20 centimetres long. The first several hundred trout are easy to scoop out, but the final dozen or so are always hard to catch. Eventually, most of the water is gone and the last fish is netted out.

Then the remaining bucketful of water is tipped out of the drum — and inevitably a little trout or two, until then somehow concealed against a rivet line or corner, escapes with it.

Late last autumn my mate Andrew and I headed to Lake Wartook in western Victoria. We've fished this lake together many times in recent years and it's a favourite water of ours, but we're not so besotted that we don't recognise its enigmatic side. Despite Wartook being relatively shallow, clear and well stocked — almost perfect credentials for fly water — there are times when you would swear there's not a fish in it. We've never completely blanked there (yet!) but we've experienced many hours of apparently perfect conditions with not a fish to be seen. At such times, against even the best advice and logic, you can start to wonder.

On this occasion we walked down to the shore under a sky heavy with cloud, the faintest breeze at our backs. Immediately we saw a trout rise, then another. We had walked in on a midge hatch that had been going on for who knows how long, and which was still going when the rain came in three hours later. At one point the wind dropped out completely, and in a slick of oily water stretching towards a distant island, good trout rose as far as we could see. 'So there are trout in here after all!' proclaimed Andrew in mock surprise, but there was a hint of honest amazement beneath the irony. And I suppose next time we visit Wartook and there's not a scale to be seen, we'll be all the more certain the trout are there, just hiding.

A Trout's Year — Autumn and Winter

ONE INTERESTING FACET of late season fishing on the mountain rivers of eastern Victoria is how quickly it deteriorates. In mid April it can be as it good as it gets for the whole year. Yet by June, a mere six weeks later, the flyfishing is all but over. For these streams at least, Queen's Birthday closing in early June is just a formality: the nature of the fishing has effectively closed the season already.

So being on the cusp of some major shifts in the annual cycles of the trout world, May is a month of indecision for me. On my local lakes in central and western Victoria, this time of year corresponds to cool though not icy water, and often the first small increases in water levels since spring. Meanwhile, truly bitter winter weather is yet to set in. It's a pretty good stillwater combination, and sure enough, around this time I often enjoy fine fishing for midging trout and smelters.

I suppose if I was reliant on trout meals to survive, I'd stick to the lakes from mid May onwards. But despite what fishing writers and guides get paid, things aren't quite that desperate! Not that I don't care whether I catch fish — I do, and preferably big ones please — but my motivation to fish is also driven by a complicated mix of other things like curiosity, nostalgia, opportunity, challenge and time limits.

It's perhaps this last factor — a closed season looming both figuratively and literally — that tends to push me towards a later-than-ideal north-east Victoria stream trip. Every couple of years, and usually during a bout of great early autumn fishing, my mates and I plan a late May trip. It's definitely a booking made with the heart more than the head. Late autumn trips to the mountain rivers are hardly ever better than passable, at least in the angling stakes.

In fact, sometimes the fishing is an outright fail. You know from what you witnessed barely weeks ago that the trout are there, often good fish in their annual prime, and plenty of them. But in the steely cold water, apparently bereft of insects or any other form of active life, the trout are glued to the bottom like inanimate decorations. This is fishing of a thousand casts, made more disheartening by the immediacy of recent successes.

Countering this grim picture, however, are the days and even whole trips when it works: fish caught in satisfactory numbers from clear, comfortable streams, set against blue skies and mountains dusted with early snow.

Regardless of the fishing standard on these trips, it's always interesting to consider what's driving the action, or lack of it. Although trout are perfectly able to cope with cold water until it actually freezes, they are essentially cold-blooded animals, whose metabolisms slow as water temperatures fall. As their energy requirements reduce, so does one impetus to feed. If food is simultaneously less active and available, that's a double whammy, and the trout are likely to adopt a lethargic attitude.

Last May, I hoped more fervently than usual to be spared the worst on our end of season trip, because I'd invited my Tasmanian guide mate Christopher along. The trouble with Christopher, if I can put it like that, is his Tasmanian guiding calendar is too full for a trip to Victoria during the best times. While he has no difficulty finding a day or two mid season to take me fishing when I'm down in Tasmania, he can't or won't let me return the favour. The best he can do is come over after the Tasmanian trout season closes at the end of April.

Since the prime stream fishing has generally faded by the time Christopher visits, I've previously chosen to take him lake fishing, and with modest success. For instance, the last time we did this he landed a 7-pound brown at Lake Bullen Merri. When discussing the upcoming trip in question, I had reminded him of these and other lake results, weighing them like an actuary against the risks of late season stream fishing. But Christopher had seen enough stillwater for the year and his heart was set on the rivers, no matter how shaky the chances. We rounded up friends Max and Dale to join us and found a riverside cabin on the Delatite River near Merrijig. I grew up in this stream-rich region near Mount Buller so at least I was familiar with all the options should things turn tough.

The cabin was more expensive to rent than we'd hoped, but it boasted several forms of heating and a decent kitchen. While a tent, a barbecue hot plate and a couple of camp chairs often suffice for comfort on a summer trip, late autumn fishing means short days, long nights and plenty of time not actually fishing. Hot food, warmth and artificial light take on added importance compared to a few months earlier.

May mornings in the mountains usually begin with one or other of the enemies of late season fishing — fog or frost. Foggy mornings may help to create pretty flyfishing photos, but for catching fish they're a downer. I don't like fishing in fog at any time of year, and the frigid blanket that descends on many a late season night and stays until midday makes things very tough. Frost is less insidious, but it steals a few degrees from water temperatures that are already lower than ideal, not to mention slowing terrestrial insect activity to a crawl. The upside is that frost usually precedes a fine day and on this trip the frosts were light enough to merely brush the edges of the narrow river flat below the cabin.

In usual style, Max and Dale prepared the sort of cooked breakfast Christopher and I normally only encounter in exotic city cafés. Mid season, I can get a bit edgy about long breakfasts, but they're ideal in May. If you take your time with a second cup of coffee, load the wood heater so it will smoulder all day, re-do your leader and pack a decent lunch, the sun should just about be on water by the time you make your first cast. So it was when we pulled up by the Howqua River, in the next valley over from the cabin.

It may be risky to tell a Tasmanian he'll never see a lovelier flyfishing river, but it's a safe call with the Howqua. Framed for most of its length by tall forest and towering mountains, the Howqua's immediate border is usually swordgrass, rock or gravel, so it never feels too enclosed or cluttered. The river's character is almost perfect — an endless succession of clearwater pools, glides, runs and riffles with hardly any dark impassable holes or unfishable rapids. At 10 to 15 metres wide, it's big enough to seem like a 'serious' water, but small enough to feel as if most of it can be covered by a fly. And if the Howqua's rainbows and browns are generally not all that big, they are plentiful.

The Howqua's fish numbers and the 'coverability' of the water were both particularly appealing on this trip, because even the best streams can hide their trout well when winter is approaching and the water temperature is just 7 degrees. Here, if we couldn't actually see the fish, at least we could probe most of the river with searching casts and drifts.

It soon became apparent that the trout were lazing on the streambed. They wouldn't move far for food or chase it, so for much of the day the secret was to fish nymphs right on the bottom, and fish them slowly. Christopher is a master of French nymphing, a technique where the angler basically trots appropriately weighted nymphs along the streambed using only a very long leader and coloured sections of tippet to mark varying depths. Under the circumstances, you'd be hard pressed to beat expert French nymphing, and the rest of us didn't. Christopher caught as many as twenty trout a session, thus giving him bragging rights around the dinner table that night, but also saving me from any jibes about poor choice of location. I persisted with indicator nymphing even when the supremacy of the French technique became obvious. Though less efficient because of the fixed depth per drift, if I fished the indicator set-up carefully and mended studiously, I could get my nymphs to the bottom in places and slow them enough to catch a respectable number of trout.

As more sunshine pushed over the ridges in the early afternoon, the air temporarily lost its bite and a few straggling mayfly fluttered down the river. In places where the bubble lines drifted slowly or curled into backwaters, the odd trout rose. Briefly I had the advantage over Christopher, being able to change my rig to dry fly with a minimum of fuss. I caught a couple of nice trout on a small Adams and felt superior about it. The opportunity to fish the dry lasted an hour or so before the high western slopes once again began obscuring the sun.

By 5 p.m. the fishing was almost over. The Howqua was shrouded in an early twilight and dew was already forming on the tea-tree, showering down my neck every time I pushed up onto the bank. My breath fogged and my fingertips felt increasingly clumsy. Our 6 p.m. rendezvous with Dale and Max was in the dark.

Along the winding gravel road on the way back to the cabin, we tallied the day's catch. Over 80 trout were landed, mainly in the 10- to 13-inch range, a handful a bit bigger. Tellingly, rainbows outnumbered browns two to one, and of the browns, only one was a mature spawner. The other mature browns — a fair portion of the trout you'd normally expect to catch in the Howqua — were either way up the tributaries doing their thing, or else too preoccupied with migrating upriver to consider eating a fly.

I've mentioned spawning already, and in terms of trout behaviour it probably cuts into late season opportunities on the north-east rivers at least as much as the other factors. Indeed, the whole spawning cycle is both a positive and negative in terms of flyfishing opportunities, not just on mountain rivers but across all trout fisheries.

Earlier in autumn, before the first big frosts and mountain snowfalls, adult trout everywhere are feeding with extra endeavour. No doubt this is partly a function of the fairly ideal conditions which prevail across virtually all antipodean trout fishing regions at this time of year; including water temperatures that are neither too cold nor too hot, long periods of settled weather and a corresponding abundance of food, both aquatic and terrestrial. An important driver of the enthusiasm with which trout feed is simply the availability of food. Trout very much respond to an abundance of catchable prey by feeding hard; conversely, they sensibly avoid burning energy hunting when food is sparse or nonexistent. Incidentally, this basic fact can be overlooked by anglers searching for more obscure and complicated reasons why the trout fishing is very good or very bad.

The enthusiasm of feeding activity in the earlier part of autumn is also linked to the forthcoming spawning season. To recap, once spawning commences trout feed much less. Instead, they devote most of their attention to migrating to a suitable spawning site, finding (and in many cases fighting for) a partner, and defending the redd from predators, including other trout. It seems likely that, on some primitive level, pre-spawning autumn trout are responding both to the need for extra calories for egg and milt production, and to store reserves to survive during a period when much energy will be expended while little is gained.

Spawning, or its approach, has other benefits for anglers. On extensive river systems the migratory pull will see good numbers of big trout leaving lakes or large rivers (where, in both cases they can be hard to get at) and moving up into more manageable parts of the system, often well before actual spawning commences. This means that, for a period, some streams will support artificially inflated numbers of outsized fish. Better yet, these trout are still interested in feeding and can be caught using regular flyfishing methods and flies, including dry flies. Rivers like the Eucumbene, which flows into the lake of the same name in the Snowy Mountains, and the Tongariro, which feeds Lake Taupo in New Zealand, are two well-known examples, but basically the phenomenon occurs on numerous streams.

During early March a couple of years ago, I was fishing the Thredbo River with my good friend and illustrator Trevor Hawkins when we came to an island where about half the river went left and half went right. We'd had a reasonable morning: three or four trout each of a pound or so on hopper patterns as a warm northerly breeze galvanised the real grasshoppers into action. As I was fishing the left side of the stream, it was the natural thing for Trevor to proceed up the right branch. The last I saw of him for about twenty minutes was his rod tip waving above the tea-tree, and then he was gone.

Nowadays the Thredbo feeds the impounded waters of Lake Jindabyne, constructed in the 1960s as part of the Snowy Mountains Scheme. But the river was very popular for decades before then, and there are good historical records of fish caught during that era thanks to an old guesthouse, The Creel, which was sadly flooded by the new lake. Essentially, The Creel's records show that the upper limit for trout caught in the Thredbo pre-lake was about 4 pounds — it's likely that this was effectively the maximum size the Thredbo River *itself* was (and probably still is) capable of growing. However, Lake Jindabyne has developed into a water able to produce much bigger trout — fish to 16 pounds are occasionally caught there, and 4-pounders are often the norm, not the exception.

Even though the very biggest trout in a population tend not to spawn, numerous out-sized lake fish run up the Thredbo, some of double figures. Significant numbers of these trout enter the Thredbo well before spawning, and stay much later. There is no question that it was such a fish, grown in the lake, which Trevor encountered around the back of the island. We were only separated for 80 metres or so, and I was becoming mildly impatient as I waited for him above the split. My side of the island had proved mediocre, with two small pools yielding just one 12-inch rainbow, and I was keen to move on. Eventually Trevor came into view, head down and stepping from rock to river rock without his usual spring and purpose. Trevor has a much better attitude to big fish tragedies than me, but even he had trouble sounding upbeat as he began his description of what had just occurred. An enormous head had engulfed his Muddler Hopper as it drifted hard against a rock face dropping into a small but very deep pool. Apparently Trevor's strike seemed good, and there was great weight on the end of the line. Then the monster brown performed a series of crocodile rolls and the fly came free. Just like that.

Trevor has taken the loss of this once-in-a-lifetime fish well. Unlike me, who dwells morbidly on a selection of would-be trophies I've lost over the years, Trevor only recalls the Thredbo giant a couple of times each season — in my company, anyway. Having shifted house twice since then, he now lives (coincidentally I'm sure) a mere 30 minutes' drive from the exact spot, not eight hours away as he did at the time. The huge trout of a few years ago has almost certainly long gone, but the small dark pool with the rock face dropping in does crop up in Trevor's dispatches quite regularly. Big trout occupy certain spots for a reason, and I wonder what else he might hook there one day.

I'm writing this in the dead of winter, and any big trout in the Thredbo, or most other rivers for that matter, are temporarily safe from anglers. Fishing regulations in most jurisdictions close rivers to winter trout fishing in recognition of how valuable this period is for wild trout to replenish their stocks. Not all the fish will be spawning at once — nature sensibly spreads the risk — and yearly variations in temperature and flow impact upon how many trout run up to spawn in a given system at a given time. But winter is certainly 'peak hour' for spawners, both browns and rainbows. Even allowing for the maiden fish, those spawning late and those that have spawned already, winter stream fishing is usually regarded as a tough task on those waters that remain open to fishing. The water is very cold, aquatic food is at its lowest ebb, and stream conditions are often unfavourably swift and discoloured. Except for a handful of estuaries and a few dedicated spawn-run fisheries, winter stream fishing in the limited places it is legal is more about proving a point or shaking off cabin fever than anything else.

As I flagged earlier though, winter *lake* fishing is another matter. From the point of view of trout behaviour, lakes offer several advantages over streams for winter flyfishing. First, the sheer volume of water present in most lakes tends to moderate temperatures somewhat, and without the extreme cold that can impact streams, trout are more likely to be active. Trout food also remains available and reasonably active through winter on the lakes — think Lake Eucumbene yabbies, Lake Bullen Merri gudgeon, and so on. As for midge or, more accurately, chironomid, these little mosquito-like insects almost seem to favour the cold on many stillwaters; I've had great midge fishing with snowflakes drifting down around me.

Winter lake fishers are also less likely to find the trout entirely distracted by spawning. As trout choose to spawn in streams and flowing water if they can, in many lakes the winter fish encountered are either yet to spawn, have already done so or are maidens. In all cases the trout are feeding and quite catchable. In fact, post-spawning fish are particularly ravenous as they endeavour to recover condition lost. Meanwhile, on lakes without stream options, even shore spawning trout seem less preoccupied with procreation, and for less of the time, and will feed and take flies much better than their stream spawning counterparts.

Lake Fyans in western Victoria is such a lake, and Max, my brother Mark and I headed there in winter with this fact but one of several in its favour. If the late season trip to the Howqua and its sister streams a couple of months earlier had felt risky (even though it had turned out well) there was no sense of pushing the limits this time. Unlike the mountain rivers, Fyans and many other Victorian lakes can be periodically too warm for good fishing over summer, but as if to reciprocate, winter fishing is more than worthwhile. I should add that if Max, Mark and I were optimistic, it was an optimism rooted in different expectations than we'd have had approaching a summer stream. At Fyans, just a couple of fish landed for the day would be acceptable, but we also hoped to encounter visibly feeding fish. And if we did catch a trout there was a good chance it would be 3 pounds or more — larger than all but the biggest river trout we could expect outside of New Zealand.

Lake Fyans lies on a plain that is astonishing for its flatness so close to the kilometre-high battlements of the Grampians, which loom up so abruptly they seem higher still. The lake itself is roughly circular and quite shallow, rimmed by a mixture of clearings and uncluttered woodland. The shoreline is an interesting mix of channels, marshes, rocks, reeds, inlets and drop-offs. The long-drowned red-gum skeletons add a certain mournful beauty to the lake, which is emphasised by the presence of the mountains in the background.

During much of the drive to the lake, Max's big four-wheel-drive was lashed by wind-driven rain. We made confidence-boosting remarks about how good winter fishing simply relies on dressing well, but I'm sure the other two were as relieved as I was when we drove out the other side of the rain band just before we arrived at the lake.

It was soon apparent that the north-west shore would offer the most shelter from the moderate wind. Wind isn't something always to be avoided on lakes. In fact, the windward shore rather than the lee shore can offer all sorts of trout-catching advantages: food dislodged by wave action, accumulated surface food, not to mention rougher water where trout are simply less spooky and more aggressive.

However, on this occasion we could opt for the 'soft' option of the sheltered shore with a clear conscience, because calm water would greatly assist us in spotting the disturbances of feeding trout. Such activity can be sparse and also quite subtle in winter, so noticing even a single boil or bow-wave is valuable. Trout that disturb the surface are almost always feeding trout, and feeding trout are catchable. What's more, trout rarely do things entirely by themselves. If you spot one trout feeding in a certain bay or over a certain kind of substrate, there is a very good chance others are doing the same.

You can even learn a lot about what the trout might be feeding on — and therefore the best fishing strategy — by the nature of the disturbance a winter trout makes. Violent slashing and crashing? Probably chasing baitfish (smelting). Slow-moving tail tips or fins in the shallows? Most likely feeding on drowned terrestrial food like worms or grubs. Tail-wagging 'rise'? Possibly taking midge pupa. Dainty, snipping rises? Sipping adult midge.

The lake looked good. It had risen a vertical half metre or so since my last visit and was now drowning thick grass and small saplings that had survived last year's brief inundation. Typically, with all the recent rain the inflow was a bit cloudy and the water had a faintly muddy tinge. But when I waded towards a submerged point I could see my boots in thigh-deep water so it was easily clear enough to fish.

With no obvious targets, the morning began with each of us searching the water with medium-sized wet flies like Yetis and Woolly Buggers — bulky, generalist patterns that gave us confidence they might be significant enough to be found by a fish. We gently worked along the shore in different directions, then carefully waded out to search slightly deeper water (the gradient of most shores at Fyans is fairly shallow). After only half an hour, Max was first to score, picking

FISHING SENSE

up a fat 2-pound rainbow while fishing a black Woolly Bugger around
a flooded corner rimmed with tussocks. As always, it was heartening
to know this 'blind' prospecting actually worked, and Mark and I kept
fishing with renewed intent.

After about an hour, a good trout shattered the sheltered water as
it attacked a school of smelt. Mark was closest and waded purposefully
toward the submerged log where the fish had moved. With his
Assassin wet fly (a rabbit fur Yeti-style pattern), he presented
repeatedly to the area, and fourth cast, a 3-pound brown hit. Two fish
in an hour — not bad.

About then light rain began to spit out of the cold grey sky, but just
as we pulled our hoods up, it stopped again. Now the only fishless
member of the party, I waded out past some head-high saplings
toward a deep narrow channel I knew, now hidden beneath the water.
I searched the channel patiently for no reward, when suddenly a fish
exploded against the saplings barely 5 metres away. My cast was there
in a second and the trout hit my Assassin on the first strip. The fish
ran straight for the saplings and there was an anxious moment as the
line caught on one. But I was fishing 8-pound tippet and I soon had
the trout out of cover and in my net. It was another 3-pound brown,
fat bodied and small headed, obviously doing well with the rising
water. I was glad to be off the mark.

And that's how our winter day continued: periods of nothing at all,
moments of excitement and the odd fish actually caught. We stayed
late in the hope of some extra flurry of action on evening, midge
perhaps or maybe even a few fish foraging in the ultra shallows. But
an icy drizzle came down off the Grampians at about the same time

as the hidden sun would have been setting. As the accompanying wind found its way along our shore, it seemed to shut down what little life there was. Before it was completely dark, Mark and I had followed Max back to the car, where he was already brewing a pot of coffee on the portable stove he takes everywhere we go.

A TROUT'S YEAR —
SPRING AND SUMMER

YOU CAN FISH streams in spring, and even enjoy good sport if you pick the right ones on the right day. But in my mind spring is still more lake time than stream time, and nearly every spring I travel to Tasmania in the hope of some special days on her stillwaters.

Last spring I headed across Bass Strait to catch up with my friend Christopher. After our successful trip to the Howqua and surrounding rivers the previous May, I was hoping we could continue the trend on his home waters.

In most places trout live, spring is a season of transition, although not a smooth one. Rather it's a wild slewing from winter to summer as if nature is struggling to restore equilibrium — a regressive snowy cold one minute; warm and sunny the next. Meanwhile, the trout (but for a few late rainbows) are mostly finished with spawning and can dedicate themselves to the business of eating and growing. Some post-spawners will choose to stay upriver if conditions are right, providing a sort of artificial boost to typical trout size, similar to the one I talked about for autumn.

For lake trout, spring must be about the most agreeable time of year. Water temperatures are usually within the comfortable range, water levels are high and, driven by extra warmth and longer sunlight hours, food supplies are booming. The whole package is helped by the fact that lakes act as a buffer to the vagaries of spring weather. Their large thermal mass tends to moderate the violent swings in temperature, and lakes can usually absorb the heavy rain events that can flood nearby streams.

For anglers though, the whole range of seasons can strike in a day, and when Christopher and I headed to his shack in the highlands, we carried everything from light shirts to high-tech parkas and mittens. The next morning we drove off intent on fishing the lakes around Bronte Lagoon, which lies smack in the geographical centre of Tasmania. However, our route took us right past Little Pine Lagoon, 30 kilometres to the east.

Now Little Pine is an extraordinary little lake. Set in a windswept subalpine bowl where only heath and tussock can survive, it is utterly unremarkable to look at. In fact, the first word that comes to mind is 'bleak'. Yet for reasons no one seems to entirely understand, Little Pine is an exceptional brown trout fishery. Despite receiving far more than its share of fishing pressure, and being subject to the most inhospitable climate, this lake (which you can comfortably walk around in a day) produces thousands of fly-caught wild brown trout every season, the vast majority of which are well-conditioned fish of 2 to 4 pounds.

Anyway, as we drove past 'The Pine' on our way to Bronte, we couldn't help but notice the relatively benign conditions — a rarity. Along the road shore, there was a 20-metre mirror before the ripple. There was even watery sunlight poking through the thin, scudding clouds. The deal was sealed when Christopher glimpsed the boat ramp as we drove past and declared the lake the highest he'd seen it that spring. We just had to stop for a quick look at least.

Never was a fishing decision more quickly vindicated. As we turned off into one of the rough car parks, we immediately spotted three trout tailing and rising over the flooded turning circle, and we hadn't even stepped out of the car!

As luck would have it, we'd struck a perfect combination of spring events. The water temperature, while still very low at just 7 degrees, was rising from an even lower base (a significant advantage which I'll discuss in more detail in the 'Temperature' chapter). The water level was creeping up too; just enough to flush a steady supply of terrestrial food (especially spiders of all things) but not so fast as to leave the trout feasting on drowned food in the depths and out of sight. Added to this were the relatively benign conditions, ideal for sighting trout sneaking around in the shallows.

It began to snow lightly as we rigged up, but no matter. Weather is always a relative thing depending on your chosen district and a few lazy snow flurries at Little Pine are nothing. If anything, the trout only seemed to feed harder. I began fishing a stick caddis under a wool indicator, while Christopher immediately took the brave step of tying on a dry fly, before striding off to the right and graciously leaving me the car park fish. To fish a dry at Little Pine, early in the season with a few flakes of snow drifting down, seemed faintly absurd, but I'd barely cast when I heard Christopher's grunt of 'Yep!' carry from up the shore, followed by the amplified splashing of what sounded like a solid trout.

I really couldn't do more than listen to all this because my eyes were fully employed. While I crouched on my knees behind a tussock, I watched four trout swim up to the normally reliable stick caddis, suspended a palm's depth below the tuft of wool just beyond my rod tip, and keep going. The fifth trout came to where the fly was and paused. I saw the white of its open mouth and I lifted into weight before the indicator had time to twitch. Soon I had a lightly spotted 3-pounder in the net. One out of five is often a good result on The Pine, but I looked up to see Christopher, 100 metres to the right, already into his second fish.

I wandered up for a chat, being careful to keep well back from any trout on the edges. 'Try one of these mate,' Christopher said, passing me a small black English hopper fly without taking his eyes off the water. The fly was messy, as English hopper patterns tend to be. (Confusingly, these are unrelated to the grasshopper flies Australians usually refer to as hoppers.) It had legs and bits sticking out all over the place. 'Just like a spider,' he declared, and in the simplistic sort of way trout seem to view the world, I guess it was. Christopher's rationale was that the real spiders plus a few other flushed creepy-crawlies were floating, not drowning — or at least not drowning straight way. Some of the swirls we saw weren't incidental disturbances, but real rises.

I tied on the little black fly and walked back to my part of the lake to look for another trout. At first I couldn't find one and I began to wonder if some small element like increasing light or the lake level stabilising had switched off the remarkable patch of action we'd stumbled upon. Then I saw ripples coming out from behind a half-flooded bush that hid the entrance to a tiny bay. In anticipation I cast the black hopper into the open water just to the right of the bush and waited. After a few seconds a good trout swam into view. For a moment it seemed distracted by something under the bush and it veered to its right, away from my fly. Then it turned again, noticed the hopper, swam up to it, opened its mouth wide and casually chomped the fly. I was so transfixed by my first rise of the trip that I barely remembered to strike — which was probably a good thing. The surprised delay gave the fish time to close its big mouth and turn down, and when I did eventually lift the rod it was well hooked. A 4-pounder this one, densely spotted like a leopard.

So the great fishing continued. The snow came and went, the sun peeked through occasionally, the trout fed busily and I caught more Little Pine browns than I could reasonably have expected. To a casual bystander, one unfamiliar with the highland climate, it might almost have seemed like winter fishing, not spring at all. But in a trout's year it was spring without a doubt, a season of plenty. The sparseness and spawning distractions of winter were already far in the past and it was time for the fish to feed with aggression and determination.

If I don't stop to think about it too much, summer is stream time. Lake fishing continues to be worthwhile and can even be at its best on some high altitude/high latitude waters. However, many lakes become warmer than ideal under the summer sun. Or at least the surface layer becomes warmer than ideal, thus restricting flyfishing to sinking lines or to between sunset and sunrise when the temperatures are cooler.

For stream trout, summer brings a combination of things that just happen to work in the flyfisher's favour. First, stream flows are inclined to drop and settle. This opens up large areas of water that were previously poor habitat for the trout because of excessive current. While the fish during spring were mostly confined to the edges, backwaters and the streambed, they can now choose from numerous 'lies' or stations. Anywhere the current delivers a steady supply of food combined with some cover is a potential place to find a trout. Those tidy diagrams in how-to-flyfish books showing trout holding in particular parts of the stream, diagrams that a few weeks ago were nonsense, start to make sense.

Meanwhile, surface insect activity — terrestrial and aquatic — reaches a crescendo in the summer warmth. Beetles, ants, termites, grasshoppers, crickets and cicadas all end up on the water by accident with a frequency that must be pleasing for the trout. Aquatic insects, especially mayfly and caddis, are as busy as they might be all year, emerging, mating, egg-laying and generally spending lots of time fluttering and bumbling about on the surface.

Without the chaos of high flows, the bugs on the edge of the trout's outside world are not only easily noticed, they are easily pursued and caught. For a while, trout become as overtly insectivorous as they are all season. As they rise gracefully all day, swaying with the pulse of the bubble line for the next drifting creature, it's as if they're designed for this more than anything. You can imagine a Macedonian a couple of millennia ago watching something similar and thinking, 'I guess I'll have to invent flyfishing.'

And as if things couldn't work more in the angler's favour, the water is warm. Not too warm hopefully, as this can put trout off their food and even kill them (more about this later), but warm enough that their metabolisms are busy and in regular need of fuel. It's not being too anthropomorphic to think of summer trout as hungry trout, and for a flyfisher that can only be a good thing.

Of course, as with just about anything in this book, summer comes with a rider or two. You can have wet summers when the rivers frequently flood and throw everything back a few months into spring mode. Or worse, you can have drought, when a lack of water can bring the streams (and the trout) to the brink. But mostly summer is a time for wet wading, active fish and lots of dry fly.

Last January saw me exploring the middle reaches of a backcountry river in the wilds of New Zealand's Kahurangi National Park, a vast tract of road-less bush and breathtakingly steep mountains in the north of the South Island. I was halfway through a backpacking trip with my brother Mark, our mate Peter and our two guides, Nick and Bruce. The sun that had beamed down generously all day had finally hidden itself behind the towering forest walls that hemmed in the river. As per the preceding three days, I'd had some extraordinary fishing. The weather was warm, the river relatively low, clear and manageable, and the trout were taking full advantage of the prolific insect activity. It hadn't been easy fishing — a cast too long or a strike too quick usually meant the end not only of that fish, but the whole pool. Nevertheless, there had been some fantastic moments, like one 7-pounder that sauntered up through about 3 vertical metres of water to eat my Royal Wulff.

That had been a couple of hours ago though. Now, with most of the river in shadow, not only was the best sight fishing over for the day but we needed to make some headway if we were to reach the next hut before evening. We'd shouldered our packs and left the fishing behind.

I don't mind admitting that by this point, trudging with a heavy pack through the beech forest, I was stuffed. The route climbed high above the river to avoid an impassable gorge, and the roar of the rapids had faded to a quiet murmur. My companions had disappeared around a corner and in the shadowy silence most of my focus was on the so-called track: trying to avoid breaking an ankle on slick tree roots one moment, then trying not to lose a boot in knee-deep mud the next. How much further to the freakin' hut?

I rounded a sharp bend in the track and the shoulder of an immense mountain loomed straight ahead. I knew the hut must be this side of it, and sure enough, a swing bridge I vaguely remembered from years earlier soon appeared. I walked carefully across the chasm below, took twenty steps through a grassy clearing on the other side and collapsed in a grateful heap outside the modest one-room building where we'd spend the night.

Isn't it amazing how the human mind works? At first I could think of no better way to end the day than lying on the grass drinking powdered orange drink, but a comfortable seat, rehydration and no pack on my back soon had my thoughts returning to the river. Here, it flowed through a gorge about 20 metres below the little flat. A casual inspection soon revealed that the slope down to the 'home pool' wasn't quite vertical, and a relatively safe path wound down to the water's edge.

The pool itself was daunting. Even with the impossible clarity of the river that fed it, much of the pool was dark and mysterious in the late afternoon shade. Towards the tail — downstream and to the left — its depth tapered to about 3 metres and every stone was visible. But as my eye wandered right, up into a gorge that was blocked by sheer walls on both sides, the boulders on the riverbed faded into a dark green blur as the depth exceeded 10 metres or more. The pool was too long to see the rapid at its head, though somewhere out of sight came the muffled roar of cascading water.

As for fishing potential, it looked limited — at least for the time being. As I sat on the rim of the gorge drinking another cup of the strange but refreshing orange stuff, I could see the odd big trout cruising deep. Back home I would have been running for the rod, but fish a few metres down in a large, slow pool are a long shot in the South Island. I wasn't giving up for good though, as I knew evening might be another matter.

The next hour or so passed pleasantly enough. There was plenty of time to wash off the day's grime in a little side creek where I wouldn't disturb the main river, then to enjoy a very civilised meal using a real table and chairs. Even the main course, a now familiar stew of freeze-dried ingredients, seemed to taste better when I didn't have to balance it on my lap.

The final task after dishes was to re-do my leader and tippet. Whatever I encountered in the home pool, I wouldn't be able to chase it far, so I re-tied every knot and replaced the 7-pound tippet with 8. For a fly, I selected an evening favourite that works pretty much everywhere, regardless of local insect variations: Doddy's Kossie Dun — big visible mast, good buoyancy and a strong hook.

With rod rigged I made my way down the steep path to the river and onto a small bedrock point. Although it was now twilight, I marvelled at how I could still make out features a couple of rod lengths below the surface. I was just thinking it might still be possible to sight a fish, when one swam by right underneath me. Caught by surprise, I managed a delayed and clumsy cast after the departing shape, but no joy.

I spent several more minutes watching for another sign of a trout without success when, out of the corner of my eye, I saw a single rise down near the pool tail. I negotiated the rocky edge until I was opposite the spot and then presented the Kossie. Almost instantly it disappeared in a rise and after a short fight I had a 3-pounder in my hands. Not bad for an after-dinner flick.

It was getting pretty dark by now and I was thinking of calling it a night when I looked back up the pool and saw another solitary rise, just off the rock promontory where I'd watched earlier. I made my way carefully back along the bank, although I wasn't confident of seeing another disturbance. Insects were scarce and an evening rise as such had not eventuated. I arrived at the rock point and looked out into the bubble line, which I could just make out in the last of the light.

That's when I saw it, not a rise but a huge dark shape, finning a few inches beneath the surface. I couldn't believe I could actually see a trout below the water when it was almost night, but my astonishment could wait. Fearing the unlikely apparition would vanish, in seconds I'd flicked the Kossie out into the bubble line a metre or so above it. The cast was a little too far to its left but it didn't matter. The shape sauntered over, and a bucket-like mouth engulfed the barely visible mast of the Kossie. I waited as long as I could stand and lifted. There was immovable weight through my acutely bent rod and the black shape just stayed there, finning with apparent nonchalance. Then it tilted down and headed steadily into the abyss below, where it was soon lost from view. I forced the rod against the trout, sideways and as hard as I dared. I tightened the drag until line only came off in painful bursts, and still the fish angled relentlessly deeper, at the same time heading upstream and further into the gorge. Soon backing appeared, the knot slowly clicking through each runner like a countdown. And then I felt something else, as if the line was being run through a pile of gravel. A few moments later, everything went limp. I reeled in the backing and line, and finally the leader. I felt for the fly, but not surprisingly all that was left was a metre of roughened tippet.

It was properly dark now and stars filled the narrow sky overhead. I climbed back up to the grassy flat, where candlelight shone from the hut windows. At the door I took a deep breath, not angry or frustrated, but unsure exactly how I could describe to my friends hooking and losing the biggest fish of my trout year.

RETRIEVES

NEITHER OF US said it out loud, but the weather was almost too perfect. It was June, and Max and I were fishing Lake Wartook. I mentioned this lake earlier. It occupies a large, shallow bowl high in the Grampians in Victoria. Surrounded by national park, Wartook is one of the oldest man-made impoundments in Australia. Early farmers and townsfolk on the fertile but drought-prone plains to the north turned to the high rainfall Grampians for a secure water supply. With horses, picks and wheelbarrows, they constructed a kilometre-long wall across the MacKenzie River, lined it immaculately with about a trillion blocks of sandstone, and created a 1000-hectare storage. So skilled was their work that, nearly 150 years later, the structure is basically unchanged.

As Max and I walked and fished our way across the wall, I silently tipped my hat to the workmanship that created a gentle slope of non-slip sandstone. Without intending to, the engineers two lifetimes ago had created just about the perfect flyfishing platform. As for the conditions, a bright mid winter sun and mirror calm lake circled by forested mountains certainly created an idyllic picture. For actual fish catching, however, we could have done with either a little ripple or some cloud cover. If trout are about when it's flat and bright, they're relatively easy to spot. But they know it and it takes only the flash of a pale palm or a careless splash to alert them to potential trouble, in this case Max and me.

The odd trout swirled as we made our way along the wall. Most were way beyond casting range, heartening to spot only in the sense that fish on the surface are usually feeding fish, and feeding fish are catchable — theoretically. A very occasional trout rose within range of the wall, though never right where we were. Max or I would jog to the spot, whoever was closer, and cover the area with a dozen casts, but only once did this result in a bump for Max and the fish was gone again in a second.

You can't be too greedy on a flat calm day with the sun well up, and even a handful of fish sighted and one hit was fair reason to stay on the wall. However, I eventually decided to split our resources and see if I could find a better offer. Leaving Max, I walked to where the shallows a few hundred metres to our right merged with a marshy foreshore near the eastern end of the wall. From there I headed north, past a group of kangaroos lazing nonchalantly in the rare winter treat of windless sunshine, until I approached a deeper channel. Here a flooded creek bed wound out from the marsh into the lake creating a tapering inlet. The water in Wartook has a slight tannin stain, so that from a distance the surface of the inlet was as smooth and flawless as a mahogany table. I was still a hundred metres away when I saw the rings of a rising trout in the middle.

I moved quickly along the soft foreshore towards the inlet, then carefully waded the last few metres so that I was a comfortable cast from it yet partly hidden behind a row of flooded rushes. Thankfully the trout was still rising, periodically snipping something from just on or under the meniscus with a clipping sound that was amplified by the stillness. I couldn't really see what the trout was eating, but the likely suspect was chironomid, the cold-tolerant 'midge' that save many a winter day's flyfishing when most other insects are dormant.

When chances are scarce, as so far on this day, I struggle with the urge to cover a rare sighted fish with whatever I already have tied to my tippet. Partly this is childish impatience — flyfishing lakes teaches you there are times to wait and times to rush, and sometimes in moments of excitement the two get confused. More rationally, solitary stillwater risers, such as the trout that was in front of me, have a history of abruptly vanishing as if they've mopped up the last midge — which is probably exactly what's happened.

Fearing this, I nevertheless showed restraint. To the stick caddis already on my tippet, I added a small black buzzer to a dropper. I looked up, ready to cast. The fish rose once more, 10 metres to my left, and then stopped. One minute ... two ... should I risk some searching casts? No, there it was again, 20 metres to my right. If it had a beat it would rise again to my right, a bit closer. Yes, and again, 2 metres closer still ... start false casting ...

The blessing of any trout that rises more than once is it gives the angler a clue to its speed and direction. And with this information you have a chance to achieve the first and most fundamental rule of presentation, which is to put the fly where the fish can find it.

I laid the sticky and buzzer out slightly beyond and about 3 metres ahead of where I imagined the trout's line to be. In the brittle conditions, where landing a fly line wasn't much better than slashing the water with an outboard motor, I dared not cast any closer. I waited a moment to let the lightly weighted flies settle, then began a very slow gathering retrieve. Jerky, darting retrieves can be useful to tease trout into taking a fly but more often a slow, steady retrieve brings a confident, no fuss take. Also, in a fishing situation where you're not certain exactly where the trout is, such a retrieve reduces the risk of inadvertently attacking the trout with your flies. If you're a trout that's made it to a decent size, you've mostly become accustomed to being the one doing the chasing. Even to your grape-sized brain, a couple of 10-millimetre bugs charging you would seem downright odd, whereas the same bugs moving along feebly are more likely to seem natural.

I twisted the line smoothly with my left hand, my right index finger ready to trap the line against the cork. I worked the flies past where I expected the trout to be and was getting ready to re-cast, when there was a steadily increasing resistance, as if the flies had snagged on one of Wartook's countless submerged logs or tree stumps. I lifted the rod tip suspiciously. Thump, thump, trout! The fish took off towards the reeds on the other side, but I was ready and applied sideways pressure to turn it.

It always feels like a small miracle when a trout takes on a lake under demanding conditions. It's partly amazement at my tiny flies finding a fish in all those vast acres of water, and I may have uttered a cry of delight. At any rate there was no further need to alert Max, because when I glanced over to the wall, his distant shape was already striding in my direction.

Well before Max had covered the half kilometre between us, I'd brought the 3-pound brown to the net in the knee-deep water, twisted out the black buzzer (it was worth making the fly change), held the trout up towards Max even though I knew it would be an anonymous blob from that far away, and released it. My friend arrived a little breathlessly a few minutes later. Of course he wanted to hear all about the first fish of the day and I was only too happy to oblige.

If the little inlet formed by the creek channel had looked good before, it was even more appealing for having yielded a fish. With only a small section of it covered so far, it seemed sensible for Max to fish the rest of it. Meanwhile, I decided to cross the apex of the inlet and explore the steeper shore off the blunt point that extended out into the main lake on the other side. I glanced at my watch and was surprised to see it was after midday; no wonder I was feeling hungry. 'I'll give the point twenty minutes or so, Max,' I called out. 'If nothing's happening we can head back for lunch.' Max acknowledged my comment with a brief wave, but didn't take his eyes off the line. Maybe he'd seen a fish.

The point couldn't have been more different to the inlet where I'd left Max. The lake here was comparatively featureless and exposed to the full strength of the prevailing westerly winds. Even under today's settled conditions, the long fetch across the full width of the lake allowed a gentle breeze to ripple the surface. And whereas the inlet was lined with reeds and presented a defined channel with a healthy margin of aquatic weed, the area off the point was white sand and silt, swept clean of all but a few hardy filaments. For hundreds of metres the shore sloped uniformly into deeper water, with no obvious channels or reefs. The only significant feature was a healthy supply of flooded tree stumps, the near-fossilised remains of a great forest that once filled large parts of the basin.

The spot was much less inspiring than the fertile, fishy looking inlet. And yet ... the tree stumps would create plenty of shelter for the nook-and-cranny loving gudgeon, a small flathead-like fish favoured in the diet of larger Wartook trout. I tried to imagine a big brown prowling through the dark stumps, hoping to ambush a gudgeon caught out in the open. It would have been an easy image to conjure up at twilight; with a bright sun overhead it was a struggle. But I had a few minutes before lunch and there was a nice ripple on the water, so what the heck? I removed the buzzer and stick caddis and bumped the tippet up to 8 pounds. Next I reached into my box for one of Muz Wilson's Emu Woolly Buggers of about the same dimensions as a typical 10-centimetre gudgeon. Pale green seemed the right colour against the light lakebed.

I could see a room-sized space among the black shapes of the submerged stumps and threw a modest cast into the middle of it. I let the fly settle for a moment and went to retrieve, but I couldn't. Before I had time to process anything much, a huge brown trout leapt from the water, shaking its head. It was by far the biggest Wartook trout I'd ever encountered and immediately I wondered if 8-pound tippet would be enough. The struggle to land it soon became a balance between applying enough pressure to steer the fish away from the many stumps without actually breaking the line. But it was too strong, and when it headed left and straight for the largest emergent stump, I couldn't stop it. I hobbled out into the lake, trying not to trip over bits of old root and wood while extending the rod tip as far as I could to keep the line from coming up against the stump. But my reach wasn't long enough. In a couple of seconds the trout had passed the outer edge of the stump, and its thuds down the line were replaced by dull weight. No!

Then a small miracle: the trout turned and swam right back again. I reconnected direct to the fish and resumed the struggle in what I assumed was open water, back in the gap where I'd first hooked it. Eventually the fish tired enough that I could bring it within netting range. It performed the classic crocodile roll that so often twists and breaks the line when the trout kicks and thrashes, but before it could complete the manoeuvre, I darted in with the net and scooped it up.

I walked back to the shore and laid the trout on its side in the sandy shallows. Fully extended, it was too long to fit in the net so its head lay submerged in the mesh while the tail third of its body extended past the rim, barely covered by the ripple. It was the perfect male brown trout, big shoulders, hooked jaw, burnt orange in colour and speckled in fine black spots.

I called out for Max at the top of my voice; he was out of sight around the other side of the point but hopefully close enough to hear me. I snapped a couple of photos of the fish beside my rod, but this was a brown I knew he would want to see in real life. While I waited, I quickly weighed the fish (slightly over 8 pounds) then thought about what had just happened.

Evidently the trout had taken the Emu Woolly Bugger virtually inert, or at best while it was settling the last few centimetres towards the bottom. Either way, a large wet fly had fooled a very big brown trout in perfect light with really no retrieve at all. I reflected that for at least the first half of my flyfishing career I'd assumed that retrieves and wet flies were essential partners: you moved wet flies, just as you emphatically didn't move dries. It was only after reading Rob Sloane's *The Truth About Trout* that I grudgingly tried inert wet fly presentations to tailing trout, and quickly discovered this was a good way — often the only way — to catch these tricky fish. In the years since, I've progressively learned that inert wet flies work beyond tailers. Humans have a habit of overcomplicating things and the urge to impart elaborate retrieves to flies under any circumstances ignores the fact that, in nature, a common prey response to danger is *not* to move.

Of course, I didn't know exactly where the Wartook brown was as it patrolled the stumps; in fact, I only had the slightest hunch there would be a trout present at all. But since accepting the value of inert wet flies so many years ago, it has become second nature to begin most wet fly presentations — even blind presentations — by simply doing nothing for a few moments. There's a chance I was lucky enough to land the fly right on top of my fish. However, a more statistically likely explanation is that the trout was somewhere in a radius of a few metres as it stalked among the old roots and stumps, and it detected the plop of my fly landing. When the fish swam over to investigate, it would have found a gudgeon-like shape, caught too far from cover to make a dash for it. To seal the fraud, the 'gudgeon' would have been quivering slightly as the marabou and emu fluttered towards the lakebed. Big brown trout are notoriously cautious, the most difficult of all trout to catch, but there was no suspicious examination before attack, no half-committed plucking at the Woolly's tail. The trout had most likely bolted over, opened a fist-size mouth, and inhaled a finger-long fly down to its gill rakers — and probably further if I hadn't drawn on the line at that point. The fly and retrieve (or lack of one) had utterly fooled the canniest of fish under conditions that favoured all its senses.

Max arrived as I was removing the fish from the net and swaying it gently in the cold water. 'My god!' he exclaimed as I lifted it briefly, which is exactly the response you want when you catch your biggest trout of the year. We took some more photos, and then watched as the trout swam off over the sand, at first distinct, then merging with the shapes of petrified wood until it vanished forever. We began the long walk back to the car, a late lunch and a pot of Max's portable stove-brewed coffee. The lake had glassed right off again and I could hear the laughing kookaburras calling to each other from the picnic ground a kilometre away.

There are plenty of other retrieves that catch trout. The 'roly-poly', where your rod is tucked under your arm to free both hands for a very fast hand-over-hand strip, can work brilliantly at times, although personally I find it's a retrieve that's tiresome to repeat if you're not getting regular takes. Some flies, like mudeye imitations, are favoured by a specialised retrieve — in this case a smooth strip, followed by a pause, followed by a smooth strip and so on. Occasionally I'll opt for a jerky strip-strip-strip-pause retrieve for certain wet flies, although I mostly find this better for estuary species like bream.

Overall however, on lakes I find myself more and more inclined toward a slow retrieve or no retrieve at all. Years ago an old angler I knew only as Ed, whom I ran into at central Victoria's Lake Cairn Curran regularly, insisted that the best retrieve was '... as slow as you can stand, then halve it'. I remember nodding politely while being silently sceptical, but I nearly always saw Ed catch a couple of fish and Cairn Curran wasn't — and isn't — an easy water. Maybe as I get older I'm no longer as impatient, or maybe I've just been convinced through repetition that slow is mostly good.

DRIFTS

I WAS FISHING the Inangahua River in New Zealand's South Island with my brother Mark. Besides having a name that passes you as a regular if you can pronounce it correctly, the Inangahua is a fine trout stream. However it's a little atypical of many other streams in the Reefton area, in that you spend a lot of time fishing the water rather than relying on sighting fish before casting. That's not only because a faint tannin stain means you can't be sure of seeing every fish; it's also due to the high number of trout present, more than enough to make blind searching worthwhile.

Don't be fooled, however, into thinking the Inangahua's healthy headcount of trout translates into easy fishing. It can actually have the opposite effect, when everything looks right yet you can't buy a trout. Knowing your fly is almost certain to be continually drifting close to fish for no response can eat away at your confidence, and if this goes on for long enough you can find yourself petulantly blaming the river for the poor fishing — a position that requires a change of venue or, at the very least, a lunch break.

Mark and I were approaching this point on a bright February morning. Cicadas were chirping noisily in the nearby forest and the odd mayfly was drifting off. Had the river been too high or a bit murky, I might have thought twice before starting the day with a dry fly. But the flow was perfect — you could cross the river comfortably if you chose your spot — and clarity was excellent. This meant a trout would have no trouble seeing the dry, and there was no disincentive to rise. From a fish's viewpoint, rising would require little energy and little risk that the 'insect' would be swept beyond reach before it could be caught.

Nevertheless, an hour's careful searching of many idyllic riffles and runs with Royal Wulffs, Stimulators and, of course, cicada patterns had produced no response. Hmmm. Then we added nymphs trailing behind our dries, but again, nothing. It was Mark who relented first and removed the dry completely. He swapped a Wulff for a tungsten-beaded Hare's Ear nymph, slip-knotting a natural wool indicator a bit over a metre above it. He then added another foot or so of slightly lighter tippet behind the Hare's Ear to which he tied a small unweighted Pheasant Tail.

For several casts nothing happened. This was the nicest run we'd fished yet: curving in a broad crescent shape; wide gravel bar on the left bank (ours); steep crumbly gravel cliff beneath forest on the other bank. The run, which looked like it was never more than chest deep, gradually tapered into a true riffle upstream. Ours was the shallow side, with steps into progressively deeper slots until what seemed to be the deepest water two-thirds of the way to the steep bank.

I was just starting to think, 'Now what do we do?' when Mark evidently found the groove or whatever you want to call it with nymphing. One cast he was just throwing his nymphs upstream and letting the current carry them down; the next he was thinking harder about how the nymphs landed, and how he managed the subsequent drift. To a casual bystander (and even to me at first) there was no difference in how he was fishing, except suddenly he had a 3-pounder leaping about on the end of the line from water he'd already covered half a dozen times. 'Ha!' Mark exclaimed delightedly, 'We just have to get 'em deep and keep them there.' He meant the nymphs. I kept back and watched as he released a very fat and surprisingly light-coloured brownie.

For sighted trout, what might be termed a 'tidy' presentation is often appropriate; the same sort of cast you'd use when trying out a new rod at the tackle shop. The leader and fly lay out straight, then the weight of the nymph alone is (hopefully) enough to bring it down to within range of targeted fish. Here, however, that hadn't been working. Apparently the fish were holding right on the bottom, either unwilling to lift at all for food or else so focused on bugs crawling or tumbling along the streambed, they simply weren't noticing anything even a foot or two above. Mark's new casts, landing the nymphs in an untidy heap and leaving a less-than-straight line on the water, might have looked terrible on a lawn, but here it sent the flies to the bottom as quickly as possible. Meanwhile the squiggle in his line bought a moment or two before he had to mend additional slack to slow the drift. Mark was ensuring his nymphs were virtually bouncing the bottom, and drifting relatively slowly too.

It proved an irresistible combination. From struggling to get a take, Mark now hooked or missed a trout virtually every cast. By the time he reached the top of the run, he'd landed eight — or so he told me later. Well before then I had already rigged up an indicator set-up of my own and headed to the next promising run.

I briefly toyed with the then new idea of French nymphing (remember Christopher on the Howqua?) as opposed to the simple indicator nymphing alternative. To recap, French nymphing utilises an extremely long level leader, jig-hooked 'bomb' and coloured leader segments allowing precise depth control. A continuous tight line between fly and angler ensures very few takes are missed. However, missed fish are a relative thing, of proportionally less importance with each trout actually landed. Indicator nymphing was much simpler to rig up for, and it would be much quicker to change again to a dry should the fish oblige later.

I caught the first trout, a 2-pounder, within three casts. Part of the trick to fishing successfully this way is concentration with every cast. The flies (and therefore the trout) will rarely do what's required if you don't make the effort. During the rest of the morning, the constant action was mostly positive reinforcement. Many Inangahua trout are, by the standards of the district, on the small side — around a pound or two — but there's also a generous sprinkling of bigger fish: 3, 4 or even 5-pounders. The possibility of these better trout, coupled with the cast-by-cast challenge of presenting the nymphs just so, meant it wasn't hard to stay focused.

Even so, there was a lot of water to fish and once or twice I found myself slackening off, subconsciously lulled by a sense that such prolific fishing would surely permit a bit of latitude. A cast that didn't quite pile; a lazy mend. But never once did such a presentation get a take. Not for the first time in my flyfishing life, I found the gap between success and failure was unnervingly narrow.

A couple of dozen trout later, Mark and I had joined up and we were fishing side by side. Any feeling of needing to catch as many fish as possible had long since been satisfied, and now it was as much fun to watch each other as to catch a trout ourselves. Losses were met with a 'Whoa!' or a chuckle, rather than a despairing sigh.

We'd borrowed our friend Felix's movie camera (Felix being our host at our Owen River Lodge base) and we took it in turns to record the action. Later back at the lodge, when we replayed the footage it was amusing to note our inability to judge the size of fish hooked. 'Looks like a beauty!' I'd exclaim into the microphone as an unseen trout charged up current, tearing line from Mark's reel. Then there would be plenty of back-pedalling as he brought a fish lucky to be 2 pounds onto the gravel. Almost all the smaller trout were muscular maiden browns, yet they reminded me more of prime rainbows in both fight and appearance.

The unexpectedly intense fishing, where a single good run could keep you occupied for an hour, had slowed our upstream progress, and lunch was long overdue by the time we approached the bridge where the car was parked. The riffle I was nymphing was tapering into a true rapid, a rubble-strewn torrent incapable of holding a trout. Mark was filming as I fished the last few metres of sun-dappled holding water. But it was only shin deep, and even allowing for the exceptional fishing we'd enjoyed until then, a last trout seemed unlikely. Then the indicator stalled and I lifted as I had a hundred times that morning. A trout exploded out of the shallows and bolted straight for the heaviest current.

When I watch our Inangahua DVD now, I notice Mark's filming during this particular fish is a little jumpy in places. But it also captures the essence of a remarkable morning that, after all, involved a fair amount of stumbling and happy chaos. Finally, I bring a 4-pounder to hand and hold it up for the camera, my smile so big it must have hurt. Then Mark pans away, for the first time showing the bridge just metres upstream, and says in a mock-serious voice that reflects a common prejudice, 'And never, ever, fish near bridges.'

It's interesting that although Mark and I enjoyed unforgettable fishing that day, we went to nymphing because we'd first failed with the dry. What's more, we would have gone back to the dry in a moment if circumstances allowed. (Actually they did and we did later on the Buller River half an hour's drive away, but that's another story.) It's the aesthetics of dry-fly fishing that give it such appeal. Even someone who's never shown much interest in fishing will usually be impressed by the sight of a trout gliding up to take a dry fly as it floats by. It's a remarkable moment that, among other things, epitomises not only the grace of flyfishing, but also the grace of trout. I know two flyfishers who long ago gave up wanting to catch their local trout, but still revel in presenting hookless dry flies to them. They've never met or corresponded, but both say watching a trout rise to the dry is the highest point of fishing existence. They might be right.

But this is getting into the foggy area of the relative merits of different kinds of flyfishing, and somehow measuring joy, challenge, anticipation and lots of other things that aren't readily weighed or compared. I will say that, at its most basic, dry-fly fishing is one of the simplest forms of flyfishing. Because you can see it the whole time, you know exactly where your dry fly is, how it's behaving, and (providing you don't turn away at the crucial moment to swat a sandfly) you also know the instant a trout eats it.

Dry-fly fishing begins to get a bit more involved, however, when we think about drift: where and how a floating fly travels in relation to the current, or more precisely, *currents*. With wet flies, we are generally representing able-bodied life: trout food that lives subsurface, and is capable of moving under its own steam, at least a little. A wet fly moving faster than the current, against it or across it, is not only acceptable, it's often more life-like. Movement contrary to the current, even subtle movement, suggests prey and often helps persuade the trout to take the fly. Slowing the drift of our nymphs on the Inangahua probably made them more appealing, not less.

With dry flies, however, we're often suggesting prey that's virtually helpless. In the case of terrestrial insects like beetles, grasshoppers and ants, they're in the water by mistake. They may manage the odd feeble kick, but fundamentally they drift wherever and however the current takes them. Even many insects with an aquatic phase to their lifecycle, such as mayfly and chironomid (midge), are more or less immobile once in contact with the river's surface. While emerging and waiting for their wings to dry, they drift at the whim of the current, and often do so again when they return to lay eggs and eventually die. There are significant exceptions to the dead-drift rule, especially in the case of the vigorous skating and skipping of many species of adult caddis. But more often than not, dead drift is *the* natural action of floating trout stream insects.

The problem with bad drift is how obvious it is to the trout. Imagine a fish feeding in a nice bubble line. All the leaves, twigs, bubbles and food drift towards it at the same pace, in the same direction. There might be periodic pulses in the current, but when this happens, *all* the floating objects obediently deviate together. Now imagine an artificial fly that travels just a little bit faster or a little bit slower, or slightly at an angle to all the other floating objects. What can seem like an insignificant difference to the angler must stand out to the trout like a bad driver on a freeway at peak hour.

The basic challenge for flyfishers is to make their fly drift like all the real food, when it's attached to a leader and fly line. Unless the current between you and your fly is moving at identical speed and in the same direction, the line has the potential to 'drag' the fly in an unnatural way. This drag probably accounts for more dry-fly refusals than anything else, so to succeed with the dry, it must be avoided.

There is another subtle yet critical element that can improve your dry-fly drift, particularly when stream flows are moderate to high, and that's simply slowing the fly's speed. Trout have a clear preference for prey that requires little effort to catch and which is unlikely to escape at the last moment. Fish occupying lies in or adjacent to swift currents rarely bother to chase speeding surface food, whether real or fraud. The energy-for-effort equation simply doesn't add up.

Now obviously, slowing dry-fly drift can't be done by artificially applying resistance — that would put us back where we started!

However, all productive trout lies in the faster water have an extra-slow strip of current nearby. Sometimes, as in the case of a well-defined seam, these strips are easy to identify. At other times they are so hard to locate that only a few trial-and-error drifts or the most careful scrutiny will reveal them.

Just before Christmas a couple of years back, I was fishing the Indi River, on the New South Wales–Victorian border. Although the flow was low by Indi standards, there were still a few places where the main channel was so narrow and steep that the current was surely too swift to offer any good dry-fly water. I was walking past one such spot when I noticed a hearty rise, right in the pressure waves. Surprised, I stared at the spot. There seemed to be nowhere a fish could shelter from the force of the rushing water, and I wondered if I'd simply mistaken the splash of a spooked carp for a trout. I was just about to turn away when a dark shape materialised in the middle of the rapid and sucked something off the top. A trout after all!

The winning fly that afternoon was a foam hopper, and I cast it expectantly above the rise. But the fly shot down the current at a quick jog, clearly too fast to even be noticed by a trout. It wasn't until two casts later that I found the slow spot, just to the other side of where I'd seen the trout. It turned out that a pale willow stump, almost invisible among the gravel, jutted off the bottom just enough to deflect the current for a metre or so. I approached as close as I dared and cast short, at the same time lifting up the rod tip to keep the line off the speeding current closest to me. The agitated water of the rapid still pushed waves over the quiet patch, but this time the fly slowed to a walk instead of a run. Reassuringly, a floating leaf and several bubbles accompanied it at the same pace. The hopper bobbed along for only a couple of seconds before a 2-pound brown cruised up and sipped it down.

I was delighted to land what proved to be the best fish of the afternoon, but I also felt slightly chastened. After all, if I hadn't noticed the rise first, I would have kept walking without so much as a cast. Still, I reflected, you never stop learning in flyfishing, and it doesn't hurt if from time to time you're reminded of little improvements you can make to your game. Even the most unlikely torrent may have a chink in its armour: not only a place where a trout could conceivably hold, but where a fly can be drifted naturally.

MICRO-PRESENTATION

I LIKE THAT some of my best fishing days are now. Not ten years ago, not even 'when I was kid, mate ...' One of the nice things about clocking up forty-odd years of fishing is that I can make comparisons between now and the old days — well, the moderately old days — with some authority. It's true there were fewer people fishing back then, but those who did fish automatically kept every trout within the legal limits, which were usually ridiculously high or nonexistent. I remember a neighbour coming home with nearly a car boot-full of big trout, and if I'm sounding self-righteous, I killed a lot of trout in my youth as well. Meanwhile, logging and mining trashed many a trout stream with barely a murmur of complaint. No one knew what 'environmental flow' or 'riparian health' meant, let alone what either looked like. The good old days? Not necessarily.

So when I say Max and I enjoyed our best-ever day on the Steavenson River on a recent mid autumn trip, it's said in a context that starts in the 1970s. The irony was that this was never a trip intent on seeking the finest possible fishing. We simply needed some photos to illustrate a couple of articles. If we caught a trout, great, but there wasn't any urgency.

The Steavenson is a pretty little Victorian fastwater that flows down out of the mountains behind Marysville. It's never quite rated up with larger streams further north and east; nevertheless, being just 90 minutes from Melbourne, it's won the hearts of many of the city's flyfishers with its good stocks of small browns and rainbows, and its classic trout stream looks.

Marysville itself was decimated by the Black Saturday wildfires in 2009, with awful loss of life and property. Fifteen months on under a gentle autumn sun, the town was dotted with the green of new growth, the gorgeous colours of the surviving deciduous trees, and the bustle of rebuilding. But juxtaposed against all these positives were the nearby ridge tops, so utterly incinerated that a monochrome scene of black tree skeletons and bare rock and earth still dominated.

Remarkably, given the destruction visited upon its catchment, the young Steavenson flowing through town appeared to be back to normal. As we travelled downstream, the Taggerty River joined it, also relatively clear and healthy looking. A few kilometres below the junction, we parked Max's car at the entrance to a friend's property. Rods were soon assembled, vests shrugged on, and we walked off down the farm track which bridged and then followed the stream. Up closer, the Steavenson was perhaps slightly more discoloured than normal, but then again it was higher than normal too after regular summer rains. As if nature felt guilty about the heat, drought and fire of the previous summer, the one just past had been the opposite. In any case, the river was certainly fishable, if not in ideal shape — or so we thought.

With strong currents and imperfect clarity, it seemed nymph fishing would offer the best chance of success. Max and I both rigged up; our visible, buoyant dries (his a Stimulator, mine a Royal Wulff) most likely to perform the role of indicator for the bead-head nymphs suspended an arm's length below, rather than main course. Max walked into the lowest pool on the beat while I started at the stock watering point half a bend upstream. By the way, the watering point existed as a function of the rest of the stream being fenced off from damaging hooves, something else you wouldn't have found in the good old days.

My first pool was a short, messy affair. The top of it was clogged by a fallen tree, while the tail split in two around a large swordgrass tussock. Dead branches above and below the water meant I couldn't cast as far upstream as I would like, while drag from the two separate tail-out chutes meant I couldn't stand back either. Ultimately my initial presentation was half-hearted, the sort of offering you make when not wanting to skip the pool altogether, but without an expectation of success.

I was so surprised to see a trout-like shape emerge out of the brown-stained water and drift back under the Royal Wulff that I momentarily assumed it was a branch that had broken free of the snag. Then the shape grew a mouth and carefully and deliberately ate the fly. In an instant I was attached to a brown much bigger than the Steavenson average, $1\frac{1}{2}$ pounds at least. With the higher than normal flow and plenty of trailing nymph-snagging obstacles to think about, it was a relief to land the strong fish on the one patch of exposed gravel I could find.

The deliberate way in which that trout tracked and ate the Wulff was all the encouragement I needed to remove the nymph. A two-fly 'each-way bet' is sometimes handy, but it's not without its downsides, including the extra level of difficulty it adds to making good dry-fly presentations — especially on a somewhat tight, overgrown stream like the Steavenson.

Max soon caught up with me and, sure enough, we soon found that the first fish was not a one-off and the trout were indeed looking up. Together we enjoyed superb dry-fly fishing until way past what would normally have been lunchtime. The trout weren't suicidal, but if you managed a tidy drift through feeding lanes where the current slowed somewhat, a rise was almost assured.

The sense I developed that morning was of the trout feeding opportunistically, with enough food of all sorts drifting down the river to have them looking to the surface, without the dominance of any one insect. Then I rounded a sharp bend to view the most perfect hopper bank I'd seen all season. Up to that point I hadn't really thought much about hopper fishing. Although there were some hoppers in the surrounding paddocks, the damp grass and lack of a breeze weren't promising for hopper action. And yet looking at this bank, it was hard to think of anything else. The bare lip of the bank, about 10 metres long, dropped almost 3 metres straight down to the main bubble line, flowing just out from what appeared to be an undercut edge. Although the bank was virtually a cliff, tussocks clung to it from top to bottom. One false move from any grasshopper and it would be in the water.

While the circumstances suggested a change to a hopper pattern, I couldn't bring myself to remove the Royal Wulff that had so far served me so well. I cast it to the upstream end of the bank and then watched expectantly as the bright white wings drifted perfectly back down the bubble line. Nothing. I cast again, and achieved a similarly ideal drift, but still no response. 'Think I should change to a hopper, Max?' I asked my friend, who was watching patiently from the other side. 'You could do,' Max replied, scratching his chin, 'But have you tried really splatting the Wulff down?' I hadn't, so I did. There was one particularly large tussock that jutted out from the bank more than the others, and I whacked the Wulff down just above it and about a foot out. A good trout shot out from under the bank and absolutely walloped the Wulff. I burst out laughing and struck, but the fly sailed harmlessly back over my shoulder.

'Try that again!' urged Max between chuckles. The response was almost identical, only this time the over-excited fish nearly leapt over the fly. It looked to be 2 pounds at least — an absolute monster for the Steavenson — and suddenly I really wanted to catch it. I cast again, but the forward stroke didn't quite come off the way I wanted and the fly merely landed on the water. There was no response as the Wulff glided past the tussock; perhaps the fish had learned its lesson. 'One more cast, Max,' I said, 'and then we'll move on.' This time the fly landed with the required plop and the fish was there in an instant. There was no mistake as it stuck its whole top jaw over the fly and pulled it under. I lifted into solid resistance; the trout leapt in surprise ... and it was off.

'Oh no!' I cried, but I was smiling at the same time. 'Three strikes and you're out, Phil,' laughed Max, and I had to agree. We continued on upriver, soon landing another trout each using the conventional presentations. No further hopper banks beckoned, but later, as we ate lunch on the tailgate, Max and I spoke about the 'three strikes' trout, and how a small alteration to presentation can change everything.

It can be useful to think of the whole flyfishing process as links in a chain, links which eventually lead to the capture of a trout ... or not. A simple chain might look like this: choosing the right destination — right conditions — fishing at the right time of day — fishing the right piece of water — choosing the right fly (or flies) — presenting appropriately — hook set correctly — fish played correctly — success!

The point is, if you take out any link in the chain, such as going to the wrong place, choosing an ineffective fly or striking too soon, you fail. Even if every other link is in place. Now on a really good day, one of those when even your beginner mate catches a fish, the links in the chain are easy to come by. Perhaps lots of different rivers and lakes are fishing well so choice of this link is not critical. A range of different flies are working, and even if you don't get the timing of the strike quite right, the trout are so committed you hook most anyway.

Conversely, an otherwise easy situation can be made extremely challenging by just one difficult link. That Steavenson trout is a classic example. Max and I were clearly on the right stream on the right day, the trout were feeding hard and at least two pretty unsophisticated fly choices were working; I'm almost certain other large generalist flies would have worked too. However, the 'three strikes' fish could only be fooled by a very specific presentation: slapping down the fly. Fly choice, good drift, good choice of spot — none of these other links was of any use without the splat. In the event it seems I buggered another link by not striking quite right on that last rise! But except for that imperfection, the story is a perfect illustration of the potential importance of what I call micro-presentation.

I think of micro-presentation as those very small things we do to the behaviour of a fly that have very big consequences for catching fish. The importance of micro-presentation is easy to ignore or overlook. It can seem illogical that something as apparently inconsequential as how hard or soft a little dry fly lands should determine whether or not a trout takes the fly. And it's true that on many occasions such subtleties are not important. The essential thing to recognise, however, is that sometimes micro-presentation *is* the missing link, the little addition to everything else that will catch the otherwise uncatchable trout.

Matching rise rhythm is another form of micro-presentation, often essential to catching trout during very heavy insect hatches or falls, both on river and lake. One October afternoon on the glorious Maruia River near Murchison in New Zealand, I was lucky enough to strike a fabulous dun hatch. The Maruia is a big, clear, rocky river that flows between a mixture of paddocks and steep forested hills. From a distance it looks like a large but accommodating pools-and-runs stream. Up close the river is more intimidating, especially when it's flowing strongly early in the season. You soon realise, for example, that the nice backwater on the far side you noticed from up on the road might as well be on the moon. It's way beyond casting range and you couldn't cross the river on horseback, let alone wade across.

Still, in a glide broad enough to dilute the force of the current, the river looked relatively manageable, and here several good fish (there are hardly any other kind in the river) rose steadily to mayfly under a hazy sky. Some were beyond reach — I soon found that wading out even a few metres reminded me of the ominous force of the river. However, three were rising within range of my bank. None refused a size 12 Shaving Brush. The first I hit too soon in all the excitement, but I waited patiently for the large heads of each of the next two to submerge before I lifted the rod. The result, after two long chases down the river, was a matching pair of 4-pound browns, dark on top but almost silvery on the sides. It was a brilliant start to the session and I would have headed back to the lodge content even if nothing else happened.

Above the glide the river steepened into an intimidating rapid, at least 50 metres wide and drowning out all other sounds with its roar. At a glance the rapid looked as if it could be summarily dismissed as a fishing option, more suited to whitewater rafting than a fly. But then I noticed a calmer strip of water on my bank, only a couple of metres wide, which continued upriver as far as a jutting rock bar that first broke the current. Having noticed this gentler strip, it only took another minute or so to notice a rising trout. I snuck down behind a manuka bush for a closer look. Whether because of hydrology or something else, there were duns absolutely pouring down the slack edge, much denser than in the glide below. In the middle of them a big snout was merrily clipping them down.

Staying concealed behind the bush, I climbed down to water level and carefully flicked the Shaver about 2 metres above the fish. Just before the fly got to it, it rose for a real dun ... then rose again just after mine had passed. It looked like a blatant rejection, but I flashed back to some very heavy Kossie dun hatches on the Indi and Swampy Plains rivers in Australia the previous autumn. There, I'd cast to trout literally rising under my rod tip and had established that it was rise *rhythm* that had to be matched to induce a take, not just correct fly and drift. Physiologically, trout can only take one mouthful at a time: they gulp down one dun, submerge to expel air and water, and then repeat the process. During a really heavy hatch of anything, on lake or stream, a trout simply can't eat everything in front of it. On a lake, its forward momentum tends to carry it under two or three bugs before it rises again; on a river, it's the current that sweeps perfectly good food right over a trout while it's still swallowing the previous mouthful. The key in both cases comes down to micro-presentation: to match the rising rhythm of the fish exactly so that your fly is in *the* spot at the moment the trout is coming up for the next insect.

That's easier said than done of course, and trout feeding heavily can also deviate off line just at the crucial moment. And that's exactly what happened with my next cast on the Maruia: my fly travelled over the magic spot at the right moment, precisely as the trout chose to take a real dun a foot to the left. Never mind. I false cast low and to the side, getting my timing back. Rise ... down ... rise ... down ... present the fly ... got him! Even for the Maruia it was a big trout, and as soon as it made it out into the rapid and headed downstream, letting the reel spin and following was the only option. Fortunately my bank was clear except for the odd flood-worn manuka, so I was able to keep up. Once I arrived at the broad glide I'd fished earlier, I managed to get below the fish, which then decided to pull away from me by swimming upstream. With the current and my rod working against the trout, I soon regained the backing and then a comforting length of fly line. It took only a few more minutes before the trout allowed me to beach it without protest — a cracking 6-pounder with big dark spots and easily the best fish of the day.

Micro-presentation, in its more or less infinite forms, is one of those elements of flyfishing that can add to the sport's mystique, which translates for some as making it all seem too hard! But I offer the concept as a solution rather than another layer of confusion. Often an apparently minute change to presentation can, quite logically, have a very big impact on the trout. There's nothing excruciatingly subtle from the trout's viewpoint about matching the rising rhythm in a heavy hatch — it is asking a lot for a trout in the process of descending beneath the water with its mouth full to eat a dry fly! Trout sees fly, eats it; trout doesn't see fly, doesn't eat it. Likewise, a trout conditioned to respond to the plop of a grasshopper is behaving in a basic, fairly primitive way to a fly that does the same thing. A slight change in force on the angler's forward cast actually equates to the difference between the dinner bell and silence to the little brains of some trout.

As I mentioned earlier, micro-presentation is not required all the time; there are plenty of situations (thank goodness!) where near enough is good enough. Nevertheless, an awareness of how crucial micro-presentation *can* be is the key. The fly that isn't working: would it make a difference if it stalled a moment longer in the back eddy? Or was sitting right way up? Or appearing half-drowned? If it was right on the bottom instead of a few inches above it? Or coming at the fish silhouetted by the sun instead of lit by it? There are plenty of occasions when any one of these things and more has helped me fool a seemingly impossible fish.

A final micro-presentation example I want to offer is how important it can be to present to trout during those moments they're 'in the mood'. Let me explain. I was guiding a relative novice, Tony, at Millbrook the other day. Overall, Tony seemed to fish better than his claimed newcomer status suggested; however, upon closer enquiry, I learned that Tony's short flyfishing career had been badly interrupted. He'd actually been taught the basics years earlier, but life's various events had ensured he'd missed out on the decent 'go' successful flyfishing requires. In fact, he'd never caught a trout on a fly.

We journeyed out to one of the lakes where I knew the spring mayfly hatch was likely to be going strong. Stalking along a steep, tussocky shore, I soon found a good fish busily taking duns as they drifted out from the flooded grass. Tony and I crawled to the shade of a solitary tree that almost overhung the trout's beat, and watched. My guest could not believe that he could actually polaroid a 2-foot trout as it swam beneath the water, gracefully picking off every dun that emerged or drifted into its path. It was a male rainbow but it behaved a bit like a brown with its tidy D-shaped beat. The trout would feed busily along the straight-edged bank into the light easterly breeze, then circle clockwise in the deeper water a few metres out to return to the start of its feeding beat half a cast behind the tree where we crouched.

It was quickly obvious to me that this fish, like many large and well-fed lake trout, had no interest in feeding downwind. It merely cruised the outer part of its beat in order to position itself to resume working upwind once again. But the sight was all too much for Tony. He couldn't bear to see the largest trout he'd encountered go uncast to, and twice he presented his Possum Emerger as the trout approached heading downwind. Fortunately they were both good casts, leading the fish by a couple of metres, but the fly was comprehensively ignored each time, as I knew it would be. 'I don't think this is the right fly,' blurted Tony after the second rejection. 'Oh, it is,' I responded quietly, 'but look there, he just ignored two real duns. He's simply not feeding when he heads downwind.' Half persuaded, Tony agreed to save his next shot until the fish was coming up the bank.

On its next lap, as the trout began heading up the shore towards us, Tony flicked a tiny but perfect cast just out from the flooded grass. Snip, the trout took an emerger 3 metres right. Snip, it took a real dun a metre from his fly ... snip, the Possum was taken without a care in the world. Tony waited for the big white mouth to close and disappear, and then lifted just like we'd practised earlier that morning. He fought the trout just like we'd practised too: rod tip at right angles to the line to absorb the lunges, line given when needed and regained when permitted. After five minutes or so, he had his first trout — a 4-pound rainbow with a stripe as bright as a fire engine. A lot of links in the chain had brought that trout to the landing net, but none more so than the fine presentation detail of offering the fly during those fleeting moments it was in the mood.

COVER

SEVERAL YEARS AGO I was lucky enough to be involved in a project to rehabilitate a degraded section of Victoria's Delatite River. The Delatite crops up a fair bit in my writings, not least because it was where, as a wide-eyed six-year-old, I caught my first trout. It's still one of my favourite rivers and I think that's only partly to do with sentimentality.

The Delatite has its beginnings between a pair of impressive 1800-metre mountains, Mount Stirling and Mount Buller. It rapidly descends between the two, until it's walled in by steep, forested slopes over a kilometre high. Here the valley floor is always damp and cool, even in the hottest summers. The young Delatite babbles and leaps between tree ferns, mossy logs and the remnants of old man-made bridges that are slowly disintegrating under the impact of floods and rot. It's a typical mountain stream: fast, rocky and cold. The trout have to manage in very swift, chilly flows for at least half the year and they're mainly small if willing — 8 to 12 inches is typical.

Below Mirimbah village the valley begins to widen and small clearings appear. The Delatite is still fast and narrow, but a bit more sunlight finds the stream and its immediate surrounds, and there are more holding pools. The trout are a little bigger, and on the best days you might catch a fish of 1½ pounds, maybe even 2. Around Merrijig the river changes again. Now it's definitely a farmland stream. There are still trees on its banks but the forests have been left behind bar the odd remnant patch of woodland. The almost claustrophobic confines of the upper valley have been replaced in just 20 kilometres by a sweeping sky and the gentlest round hills. The Delatite still bubbles along a rock and gravel bed complete with cascades, riffles and rapids, but there are substantial pools at regular intervals. This 'bigger', more fertile river and surrounds changes the game significantly for flyfishing. The trout are larger but less desperate and in less of a rush, taking their time to pick food from the lazy bubble lines and gentle riffles, even cruising the stiller pools like small lakes. A flyfisher must work more carefully and thoughtfully if they wish to catch these mid Delatite trout.

Notwithstanding the agricultural surrounds, these middle reaches of the Delatite mostly provide good habitat and plenty of cover and shelter for the fish. However, there's one stretch that was intensively mined for gravel many years ago, leaving a broad featureless bedrock channel not much more inviting to fish or fishers than a wet freeway. At normal flows the river here barely had enough depth to support a fingerling. I remember fishing near this stretch as a boy and automatically making the half-kilometre detour to regain worthwhile water above the scar.

It was pure fluke that, decades later, a couple of friends ended up acquiring the properties surrounding this mined stretch of river. To cut a very long story short, we set about finding a way to restore the worst-affected part, and with the help of a number of agencies and fisheries experts, that's what happened. The channel was narrowed and deepened to something like its original state, boulders were returned and trees and shrubs were planted to provide shade and, ultimately, when they lost branches or toppled over, more in-stream structure.

Local fisheries scientists surveyed the section before and after the work. The number of trout and other fish present increased dramatically in the 'after' survey, with the biggest change from an angling viewpoint being the appearance of larger, catchable-size trout. Such trout had been basically absent in this part of the Delatite for decades.

This increase in size and numbers of trout happened without any help at all from artificial stocking, something which surprised some of my fishing mates. But it was no surprise to any of the fisheries scientists involved. One, my friend Paul Brown, has visited stream habitat improvement projects in the United States that have increased trout numbers ten-fold. And remember, it's purely improvements to structural habitat we're talking about, with flows, water quality, stocking rates and so on unchanged. You could simplify to say trout numbers and size can be drastically improved merely by giving them decent places to hide; by, if you like, making them feel safe.

All this is interesting in its own right — or it should be. But the ramifications for actual fishing are just as important. If artificially improving structural habit has such an impact, then what does this say about where we should fish, where we should concentrate effort?

Trout love cover and being aware of this simple fact has caught me more fish than I can hope to count. Of course, flyfishers mostly don't like cover, not intuitively anyway. Overhead structure makes casting and fly presentation more difficult, while subsurface cover like weed and snags can catch the fly. Deliberately seeking clutter doesn't come naturally, but if you can force yourself to do it, fish-catching opportunities improve immeasurably. Some days, the presence or absence of cover is the defining factor — you catch fish with it, and you catch nothing without it. White and black.

Are trout found away from cover? Absolutely. For instance, many of us have caught fine trout cruising broad, shallow lake flats in bright sunshine. However, both lake and stream trout have, overall, a preference for cover in its many forms.

'Many forms' is an important concept here. Broken water, shadow and turbidity can all help to hide or camouflage a trout just as well as a boulder, undercut bank or a clump of weed. One day I was fishing a rain-clouded stretch of the Thredbo River with another fisheries scientist mate, Steve. I was complaining about the poor visibility when he rolled his eyes and said, 'Phil, trout *like* a bit of colour in the water. Predators can't see 'em, and meanwhile, they can sneak up on their dinner.' Just as Steve finished speaking, a trout smashed into some unfortunate life form — probably minnows — in a backwater on the far bank. 'See what I mean?' he smiled, vindicated already. 'Flyfishers enjoy clear water because it looks pretty and they can see the trout better.' He started wading out into the swollen current, obviously intent on attempting the 20-metre cast to the backwater. 'But trout don't have any interest in pleasing or not pleasing flyfishers — they just like what they like.'

Steve had made a good point, and one that's worth remembering when you're having second thoughts about, say, fishing into the wind or being a right-hander fishing the right bank on a forest stream — not to mention when confronted by discoloured water.

Weed is one form of cover often encountered when trout fishing, including at Loch Cameron, a small, circular lake which lies in a snug hollow surrounded by the vast and almost treeless high plains south-east of Mount Cook in New Zealand. It was a bright blue December day and, unusually for the area, utterly still. The lake was a perfect mirror, reflecting every snowdrift and dark crag on the Ben Ohau Range in the middle distance. I could see the trout easily, mainly browns of 2 to 4 pounds as they cruised the silty inshore margin nervously. And that was the problem: the fish were so jittery they would flee in fright from even a dark green, inert damsel nymph, usually a winning fly on these high country lakes.

Finally, after stalking the shore for half an hour for no result other than several alarmed trout, I came upon some clumps of weed. Not a dense matt, more a miniature aquatic woodland. The weed was dark and mottled and I had to stare hard before I eventually spotted a fish weaving between the gaps. How different was its behaviour to the other dozen or so trout I'd sighted up until then. No anxious darting, no freezing on the bottom. This trout cruised confidently about a metre down, periodically accelerating and flashing its white mouth as it ate something. I waited until it had swum past me, then cast the damsel nymph, which dangled an arm's length or so beneath a Royal Wulff, into one of the larger holes in the weed. The trout turned just at the edge of my vision, and then came back towards me. It disappeared for a moment, and when I next saw it, the trout was charging into the hole, taking the nymph so hard that the Wulff made a swishing sound as it took off after it. A 3-pounder was soon in the net.

When I moved on, I still cast to any trout I saw out in the open (you never know) but it was only around the weedbeds that I was able to catch two more.

The pattern has repeated itself time and again on lake trips, especially during bright, calm conditions. When things look desperate in the open water, I can usually find salvation where there's cover. In addition to weed, things like boulders, rushes, flooded tussocks, drowned trees and fallen timber all provide ideal structure for trout to cruise with confidence. By the way, dense weed or really thick flooded vegetation can provide too much of a good thing and is often as barren as the open flats. I'm guessing hunting opportunities are poor where trout can't move freely, and where a shrimp or water beetle only has to give a kick and it's safely out of reach.

If cover can be important on lakes, its value is amplified on streams. Except on the mightiest rivers, stream trout live a more exposed existence than lake trout. Put it this way, many a lake fish could easily go its whole life without seeing an angler, but only a trout on the most remote stream could expect the same. Streams are generally more confined and shallow, and trout know it — or should I say they seem instinctively aware of their vulnerability in that primitively effective, survival-driven way of lower order animals. Stream trout might stray from cover if there's an absolute feast on offer. However, most of the time, they want to be where those nasty predators in the outside world have difficulty seeing or reaching them.

I've covered a few such times and places already, and I could list pages more of them and still smack my forehead when this book comes out and say, 'Bugger, forgot to mention foam rafts' or something. So perhaps I can put it another way. If you're on a stream and you can cast as if in the middle of a football field, while being able to see into the water well enough that you would spot any trout on the bottom with your eyes half closed; then you probably *won't* spot a trout, or at least not one you can catch.

It was February on Victoria's Goulburn River. John fishes this water a couple of times a week during the season, and he all but guaranteed me amazing fishing among the willows and tea-tree if I made it up while the river was fairly high. I reckon promises like that are testing the fishing gods, but I came up anyway. It was an oppressive day, humid and still and I couldn't wait to step into the river and wet wade.

Cumulus clouds began shooting up from late morning, slowly filling the sky so that any sun-assisted polaroiding was soon ruled out. It didn't matter. Most of the trout, both the dedicated willow grub feeders and those with more varied tastes, cruised under the willows and spotting was actually easier without the mottled shade sunshine would have produced. Apparently the fishing gods were feeling magnanimous, for bar having to wipe the sweat off my polaroids every few minutes, conditions were ideal. The trout were feeding hard, and as with most fish near plenty of structure and cover, they were relatively carefree. Some Goulburn trout have eyes in their tails, but I guess in the willows, upright anglers, arms and rods just blend in. I don't own a rod short enough to be perfect for this sort of fishing, so we took it in turns with John's 6-foot, 3-weight. Actually John mostly spotted while I fished, despite my occasional half-hearted protest. There was no need to cast far, just to present (and strike) in a confined space, hence the short rod. More than half my takes came to bow-and-arrow casts, the rest to a single flick.

It was brilliant fishing, some of the best I've ever had on the Goulburn. I landed four trout over 1½ pounds, the biggest closer to 3, and I missed or lost many more. It was up close sight fishing at its finest, sport you'd travel a long way to better. All the fish I hooked took a willow grub imitation or a Wee Creek Hopper — the real grasshoppers were abundant along the grassy edges, even where the willows encroached.

A couple of fussy fish nudged a foam beetle, although 'fussy' is probably unfair; my less-than-perfect first presentations seemed to make those particular trout wary. Even fish feeding hard and close to cover aren't completely blind to danger. When you're virtually standing on top of them and the first cast or drift isn't quite right, you normally witness the subtle change from top gear to something a little more subdued. The trout aren't exactly spooked, but there's a bit of caution in their behaviour that wasn't there minutes before. Any sight fisher — from the Oreti to Olive Lagoon — knows just what I mean.

Late in the afternoon the towering clouds began to emit faint rumbles and rain curtains started to form in the middle distance. A combination of poor light and the threat of being caught in a storm persuaded us to call it a day. On the long walk back to the car, John and I talked about maybe staying on to see if evening produced a termite fall or some such. But occasionally, just occasionally, a fishing day is best finished before the clock says it has to, and an icy soft drink by the bridge was a more than fitting end.

That Goulburn session emphasised the value of cover to good flyfishing. The Goulburn is possibly the most heavily fished trout river in Australia and, as any regular knows, the larger trout especially become extremely spooky and fussy. Indeed, on that same day with John, I did locate a couple of nice browns in more open water; water where I could cast properly and I didn't have to think about where to place every footstep. But these fish might as well have been in another river to those in the trees. One bolted in fright from 10 metres away even though I was standing completely still. The other came up to my willow grub (the exact fly that had fooled several nice fish in the thick cover), looked at it carefully, then fled as if it were about to explode. After that it was almost a relief to push and wriggle my way back in among the branches. Maybe I couldn't cast as freely as I'd like, but when a trout swam right under the log I was standing on, busily chomping and swirling, I decided that for now at least, the joy of long graceful casts was overrated.

CONDITIONS

ONE INTERESTING ELEMENT of guiding is that you occasionally find yourself persevering in conditions when, if fishing alone, you would have headed back to camp. Rather than trying to put a guest onto fish, you might be tending the fire, tying on a new leader or sorting out your fly box.

But there are some advantages to continuing to be out on the water when the proverbial book says it's a waste of time. For one thing, it inevitably leads to a rethink of when trout are likely to be catchable, and when they're not. For example, it turns out you actually can have worthwhile fishing when the water's supposedly too warm or too cold, when you can't see your toe in calf-deep water, when the barometer's falling, or when the wind is from the east, and the fishing is, according to the saying, the least. In some ways this can feel like illumination in reverse — the lights in your head are flickering off rather than on — except the lights weren't real to begin with.

Last winter I tested the limits of when you should go fishing and when you really shouldn't. It was a guiding assignment. I was looking after Ed, who has been coming to Millbrook for years, and his brother Steve. Ed learned to flyfish at Millbrook, graduating from beginner to proficient angler in no time. He's quietly spoken and independent, the kind of angler who can end up catching several good trout without anyone noticing.

After numerous attempts, the brothers had finally managed to match a couple of days off to go fishing. Ed was convinced Steve would love flyfishing, and besides spending time with a brother he saw too infrequently, Ed obviously hoped to convert him to the fly.

The boys arrived from Sydney on a cold, gusty Friday afternoon in July. They put in an hour or so of fishing on their own before running out of light and retiring to the cabin. I arrived at the cabin after breakfast the next morning. The weather forecast was abysmal, with the most worrying element being a Severe Weather Warning for damaging winds in excess of 100 kilometres per hour. Even early in the day, the branches rattled as I walked to the cabin's front door and clouds raced overhead with ominous speed.

It wasn't as if the forecast conditions were unprecedented. The Millbrook area lies close to the crest of the Great Divide and it lacks steep, sheltered valleys. So most years, we experience two or three days when the best sort of fishing is indoors via a good book or magazine. Once in a while such days have clashed with guiding commitments. Usually those occasions had coincided with day trips booked by local flyfishers. It made sense to everyone to postpone until things settled down a bit.

The problem this time was that my guests had travelled a long way to be at Millbrook — over 1000 kilometres in fact. What's more, having been privy to the planning, I was aware how many attempts it had taken for two busy brothers to find two days to spend together. Clearly, suggesting they 'pop up next week when the weather's better' wasn't an option.

There was always a chance Ed or his brother would themselves recommend we cancel. However, from the first day I met Ed I sensed his quiet demeanour concealed a great determination to catch fish. Sure enough, when I knocked on the door, Ed greeted me wearing his fly vest and beanie. Meanwhile Steve cheerfully shook my hand and voiced his enthusiasm for the day ahead. I couldn't tell whether his optimism was based on innocence or hope, but I smiled back as a good guide should and said words to the effect that anything was possible in flyfishing — which, in my defence, is true.

In the lee of the dense plantation that lines the north shore of Cabin Lake, we found some shelter from the gathering gale, enough to get Steve casting and for Ed to have a shot at a sighted fish or two. But then the wind began to blow small branches onto the water and the nearby trees went from merely waving to bending like 12 weights with sailfish on the end. I decided that, if nothing else, we needed to be somewhere safer.

Safer meant a place devoid of trees or anything else that could fall on us or hurtle through the air. The fairway-like surrounds of Bluegum Lake certainly ensured this, but of course at the same time offered no shelter at all. When I pulled the car up by the water, the wind made a droning sound in the roof rails I'd never heard before.

The normally clear water of Bluegum looked like the Shipwreck Coast on a bad day. Waves half a metre high smashed against the windward shore, washing in chunks of bank and grass and turning the whole lake a milky grey.

Usually, when I guide or fish, I manage to maintain at least the belief that trout are going to be caught. However, as we struggled to stand up in a gale that a nearby weather station measured at a steady 90 kilometres per hour, gusting to 110 kilometres per hour, there came a point when I inwardly accepted we were just going through the motions. Still, there was a certain strange fascination in not only being outdoors in such conditions, but actually trying to catch a trout. I watched mini waterspouts spiral across the lake, saw sheets of whitewater lift off and drench the ground 10 metres from the bank. A few kilometres away at my brother's place, a garden shed was blown out of his yard and five trees were torn up. At one stage I fumbled a weighted Woolly Bugger and it blew out of sight.

I've never felt at such a loss while guiding, at the same time understanding completely there was nothing else I could do. After an hour or so I decided our hopeless efforts had gone on long enough. I suggested we head for Buninyong Lake, as much for the fifteen minutes of respite in the car as for any likely improvement in the fishing.

Then, as we arrived at the new lake, the wind eased just a little. On any other day we would have cursed the blustery gusts that flapped our jackets and pushed against the car doors as we forced them open. But a lake without tornadoes, a lake with at least patches of clear water, was a treat after the previous hours. I told Ed to work a Magoo back fast across a shallow bay with the wind behind him. Ten minutes later

Ed came into view while Steve and I searched a steeper shore, his rod bent hard and a silver 5-pound rainbow ripping through the waves. Shortly after Steve hooked and lost a comparable fish — a tough deal on a tough day, but at least he felt a good trout on the end.

Night descended with the thickening cloud and soon after we retreated to the cabin. If a warm fire and solid refuge from the wind had seemed appealing when we first headed out many hours earlier, it was paradise on earth now. We sat in blissful silence for a while, sipping hot drinks and staring into the flames. It was Steve who spoke first. 'Well, Ed, you were right,' he announced without a trace of sarcasm, 'This flyfishing is bloody great!'

That Millbrook day stands out as the worst conditions I've consciously persevered in. Of course I've been *caught* in extreme weather while fishing several times: a blizzard on the Bogong High Plains comes to mind, as does a tornado I barely escaped on the Mitta Mitta River. If you fish for long enough, sooner or later you find yourself too far from the hut, tent or car when a storm descends. This most often occurs when the fishing is so good you kid yourself that the storm in question is a few minutes further away than it really is. Either that, or you're so absorbed in the small area of water in front of you, you fail to notice things are about to deteriorate until the first fat raindrop smacks you in the back of the head, or a big snowflake drifts past your nose. But to clarify the distinction, until that day with Ed and Steve, I had never actually kept trying to catch a fish (or help others do the same) while in the thick of extreme weather.

Flyfishing conditions might be considered in two parts: what could simplistically be described as their effect on angler comfort and their effect on trout behaviour. The first part is largely subjective, but is no less important for that. Where conditions cross the line between passable or not will depend on things like how well you can cast, how you're dressed and — let's be honest — how badly you want to catch a fish compared to, say, staying warm and dry. There is no right or wrong answer here. I will only observe, as many writers have before me, that ultimately we're not at war with the trout. Once flyfishing ceases to be enjoyable, my advice would be to stop and do something else for a while.

The second part, about how the trout themselves respond to various conditions, is more defined, although it's still the subject of much myth, misinformation and misunderstanding. With this in mind, in the next few chapters I'll look at how different elements impact upon trout and trout fishing.

WATER TEMPERATURE

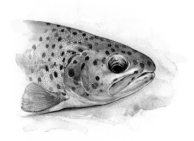

THERE ARE FEW natural variables more significant to trout fishing than water temperature, and yet this element is among the most widely misunderstood by flyfishers. That's if it's not ignored altogether. Trout are rightly classified as cold-water fish. They can tolerate chilly water up to the point when it actually freezes solid. Short of being set in a block of ice, the only negative effect trout suffer as the temperature drops towards zero is a slowing metabolism and therefore a reduced demand for food — more a problem for fishing than the fish, which we'll cover later.

On the other hand, water that gets warm enough will eventually kill trout. Being more or less cold blooded, their metabolism speeds up and demands extra oxygen as the water heats, at the same time as the dissolved oxygen content is declining in response to increasing temperatures. The oncoming collision is clear: at the very time a trout's demand for oxygen is increasing, its availability is decreasing. At some point, the combination will prove lethal.

As I was growing up, the trout and temperature thing seemed reasonably clear. The books I read disagreed a little about the 'ideal' temperature range for trout (it was somewhere between 12 and 18°C, give or take a degree). But they were unanimous that anything over 19°C was a problem and anything over 20°C left the trout concerned only with survival and uncatchable. At 23°C they all died. This made perfect sense. Even the most ideal trout regions, from Montana to New Zealand, occasionally suffer extremes of drought and temperature, and within a few years of taking up trout fishing I'd already witnessed the sad spectacle of trout perishing in low, warm streams and lakes.

Given the profound impact of high water temperatures on trout fishing, I'm not sure why it took me (or any of my fishing mates for that matter) so long to invest in a thermometer. Maybe it was the misguided belief that dipping a finger in the water could tell if it was too warm or not. In fact, finger-dipping, wet wading and so on is only useful for taking a rough punt on *relative* temperature: even 25°C water will feel cool on a 40°C day.

So when I eventually did invest $10 in a thermometer, I was in for a surprise. It turned out that much of my summer fishing occurred on streams running at 20°C or more. As for lakes, surface temperatures of 23 or 24°C still produced trout.

It was two trips to the Indi River in the summer of 2001 that really shook the whole trout and temperature thing for me. I've mentioned this river already and it's actually the upper reaches of the Murray River, that iconic waterway which forms the border between Victoria and New South Wales. The Indi is a truly lovely trout stream, fast and clear, bearing little resemblance to the broad and murky red-gum-lined river most people know. However, by the time the Indi exits its mountain gorges into the open flats of the Biggara Valley, it is only a few hundred metres above sea level, and it can heat up alarmingly during hot summers.

When Ray, my Sydney friend Mark and I arrived on a mid January evening, I was quietly cursing our luck. I'd watched the temperatures leading up to our trip and they'd been consistently peaking in the high thirties. Worse, the nights hadn't dropped much below twenty. Trout water can withstand bursts of heat — it takes a lot of energy to warm a reasonable-sized lake or stream — but cumulative heat like this is a real problem. It was Mark's first trip to the rivers this far south. I'd tried my best not to talk things up too much, but I'd had brilliant fishing on the Indi just a month earlier and I think I may have hinted that the fishing in January could be pretty good.

When I opened the door of the old riverside farmhouse where we were staying, the stifling heat inside confirmed my fears. Reasonably insulated buildings that have been shut up for a while are a fair indicator of local water temperature. The figures mightn't match up exactly, but put it this way: if your breath fogs when you walk into such a building in late autumn, I'll bet the nearby stream temperature is in single figures. On the other hand, if your first reaction is to open all the doors and windows — as in this case — you'll be lucky if the river is running at less than 20°C.

I dipped my hand into the lukewarm Indi, holding the thermometer under for a minute or two. I lifted it out, shook it and submerged it again, but I couldn't make the red spirit drop any lower.

'What's it say?' Mark asked brightly. At that time he was still fairly new to flyfishing and he probably assumed taking the water temperature was just another odd ritual he'd soon comprehend, like dusting dry flies with Gink. '23.5 degrees,' I replied, trying not to frown. 'Oh,' said Mark. I doubt he really knew back then what a 'good' water temperature was, but he was aware that you couldn't catch trout in, say, the Hawkesbury, Sydney's nearest substantial freshwater river and several hundred kilometres closer to the tropics than the Indi. 'Isn't that a little warm?' he continued. I explained that, yes, it was, but that hopefully the Indi would cool down to a reasonable temperature overnight. I hoped I was right, but secretly I doubted it.

Well, that trip my worst fears were realised water temperature-wise, but blessedly, not when it came to the fishing. It was great, better even than December. This was summarised in my diary, which I have in front of me now. The original account has lots of underlining and exclamation marks which I'll spare you, but the following is otherwise lifted straight from its pages: '*Generally excellent fishing, despite water being warm most of the time. Best day, temp. ranged from 21–23.5°C, yet fishing got better as water got warmer. First 3-pounder caught in flat water in 22.5°C, mid pool.*' Under 'Fish Caught', I wrote: '*71, even mix B & R* [that's browns and rainbows], *including 2 x 3 lb. Browns, many 1–1½ lb, 2½ lb.*'

Okay, I'm not sure exactly what that very last bit means (it's unlikely there was a strange absence of trout between 1½ and 2½ pounds), but to be fair it would have been written late at night after a hot, busy day. Looking back over years of diaries, I notice that early season and late season, when the days are shorter, my comments tend to be quite long and lyrical. No doubt I'd come off the water at a civilised hour, had a good meal and was more than happy to sit by the fire and complete my journal properly. If I was away fishing with friends, they no doubt gave me some gentle grief about my conscientiousness; perhaps tinged with a little guilt they weren't doing the same.

Midsummer comments however, like those above, tend to be sparser. I can picture myself fishing the evening rise until at least 9.30 p.m., then finding my way back to camp by torchlight and gulping a hastily prepared meal. By the time the dishes are done, it might be nudging 11 p.m. Filling out the diary at close to midnight after a long day feels more like homework than anything else. The presence of any comment at all beyond bare facts and figures is likely to reflect something out of the ordinary, driven either by excess nervous energy or the knowledge that some events simply must be noted while the detail is fresh. This was clearly the case here, and ten years on we get the message: terrific fishing despite warm water.

If I needed any convincing, I was back on the Indi again in February. This time the water was even hotter. But the action, particularly grasshopper action, wasn't diminished. Toward evening, in the choppy head of a favoured hopper pool — one lined by high gravel banks topped with tussocks — Ray caught a $3^{1}/_{2}$-pound brown on a Rick Keam Polyhopper. It was our best Indi trout that summer, and the water was 24°C.

I don't need to go back a decade to find subsequent examples of temperature-tolerant trout. In fact every year I catch trout in water of at least 23°C, occasionally as high as 25°C. My friends who carry thermometers experience much the same. If most Australian trout anglers measured the water temperature regularly over summer, they too would discover they catch plenty of active, healthy trout in water warmer than 20°C.

So how is it such a discrepancy can occur between the accepted wisdom regarding trout and upper temperature tolerance, and the reality? Seeking an answer, I began researching the topic several years back, and called on friend and fisheries scientist Paul Brown to help. The result was an article we published together in *The Flyfishers Annual*, Volume 7, back in 2002. To simplify a little, one thing that became apparent as we delved into the subject was that trout will tolerate (and even feed) in high water temperatures *if* they have an opportunity to acclimatise to warm water first. Take a trout from a 13°C stream and place it straight into 23°C water and it will be in trouble. However, expose a trout gradually to warming water, as happens on most mainland Australian trout streams and lakes every summer (not to mention many trout waters in other parts of the world), and they can adapt up to a point.

A parallel explanation is that certain environments select, over time, for trout with the right genetic make-up to cope with warm water. When temperatures approach the lethal limit on a particular water, 100 per cent trout mortality is quite rare. Even among trout of otherwise identical age, size and condition, some succumb in hours, some in days, and some make it through. On several occasions over the years I've seen favourite waters hit by relentless heatwaves and low water, and witnessed dead and dying trout by the hundred. The assumption at such times is that all the trout have perished. However, when kinder conditions return, there are usually some trout left, larger than life so to speak. With a relatively short time between trout generations, even a few decades of selective pressure must favour the genes of the warm water survivors.

Another consideration in the warm water equation is that trout can use areas of cold water to enable brief warm water sorties. Being mostly made of water themselves, trout can cool their bodies down by spending time in cold water. Once chilled, the fish can then spend several minutes in warm water before needing to retreat. The greater the trout's mass, the better the technique works. This 'recharging' tactic applies most obviously on lakes. In summer, stillwaters are often stratified and, only a few metres down, they usually retain a layer of water several degrees colder than the surface, as any kid who spends summer swimming in a farm dam will tell you. If the food reward is sufficient, trout will cheerfully travel up from this cooler water to feed in a surface layer that would be warm enough to kill them eventually.

Summer mudeye migrations are great drivers of this sort of fishing. On many warm muggy evenings at lakes like Fyans in western Victoria and Eucumbene in the Snowys, I've waded into the bath-like shallows and caught plenty of trout as the mudeyes swim determinedly for the shore. Clearly, the lure of big, easy-to-catch dragonfly larvae is more than enough to pull the trout out of the cool comfort of deeper water — at least in bursts. Typically these nocturnal mudeye feeders are decent fish of 1 to 2 kilograms, sometimes more, and their large mass gives them plenty of time to feed (and the angler plenty of time to cast) before they need to slink back to the trout equivalent of some air-conditioned comfort to digest dinner. Trout in warm streams with access to cold inflowing tributaries or springs can perform much the same trick.

A final variable is overall water quality, including dissolved oxygen content. Obviously pure, well-oxygenated water that's approaching the upper temperature limits is always going to be a better place for a trout than water of equal temperature that is stagnant or polluted.

None of this means high water temperatures can be ignored when flyfishing for trout; only that the definition of what is too warm can vary by several degrees depending on a whole range of circumstances. The important thing to note is that many texts underestimate the tolerance of trout to warm water. So here's the reality: trout in water of reasonable quality, that have evolved in warmer water or had time to acclimatise to it, or which have access to cold water nearby (or a combination of all the above) can provide good sport well beyond the commonly accepted maximum temperatures.

To go to the other end of the scale, the coldest water I've ever fished was on the Victoria River, south of the Bogong High Plains. Oddly enough this wasn't in the depths of winter, but in mid May. It was an unusual autumn. Helen, the expert horsewoman whose big warm house Trevor, Dale, Max and I were renting in the Bundarra River valley, had been caught by a blizzard while out riding a few weeks earlier. As we waited for a big pot of soup to warm on the cast-iron stove, she described her adventure. 'Forecast was for a few snow showers,' she explained, 'but when we woke up in the hut the next morning there was half a metre of the stuff outside; more in drifts on the track.' Helen's lived in these mountains a long time. She took a sip of her tea and laughed. 'It was heavier snow than we get midwinter some years,' she continued, then added with bush understatement, 'Took a bit to get the horses through it and back home.'

In the moonlight we could see the white gleam of the unusual May snowpack on the ranges at the head of Helen's valley, still unmelted on the southern slopes. The fishing since we arrived had been quite tough, not helped by a burst of cold rain which caused some rivers to rise and discolour, the effect exacerbated by the input of icy meltwater. Although May is, as I've mentioned before, too late in the season to expect miracles, this trip had a hard edge to it even by the standards of the month.

As we enjoyed an endless supply of pumpkin soup and homemade bread, the talk around the table turned to the next day's fishing, and that's when the Victoria River came up. This pretty little stream winds through a mix of subalpine snowgrass and snowgum woodland. As it's at an elevation of around 1100 metres, we'd originally deemed it too high and therefore too cold this late in the season. However, it was also likely its catchment had missed the rain that had hit the more northern streams, so if nothing else the Victoria's flow would probably be clear and gentle.

The next day dawned sharp and frosty. In the paddock below the house the horses steamed in the first rays of sun. We had to take care not to slip on the ice-glazed stairs as the car was packed.

By 9 a.m. we were topping up with fuel in Omeo, halfway to the Victoria. The sun was beginning to melt the frost on the iron roofs lining the main street, and water gurgled down drainpipes. Here and there people in the street stopped to chat, lingering in the warm rays. Although the air temperature was still only a few degrees, the solar radiation exaggerated the heat and the four of us congratulated ourselves on our decision to visit the Victoria.

It was a little while since I'd last fished the river and it took me two attempts to locate the old track which wound through the snowgums and down to my favourite stretch. The stream looked idyllic as it twisted lazily through mottled sunlight, riffles of fine gravel joining tussock-lined pools. I walked down to check the clarity (good) and immediately scared a foot-long brown trout, which bow-waved from its position in a pool tail to the safety of a sunken branch. Obviously the stream had avoided the rain and, whatever other challenges we faced, finding trout to cast to would be straightforward.

Max and Trevor headed upstream, Dale and I down. So long as you keep an eye out for wombat holes, this subalpine woodland/snow plain country is easy to negotiate, and it was straightforward to shortcut across the Victoria's many S-bends while staying well back from the water. In no time we had more than enough stream to keep us busy for the three hours until we were due to meet back at the car.

In the pictures I took that day it almost looks like late summer. The sun is shining and the sky is a deep alpine blue. The closely cropped grass on the little river flat is green but the tussocks are straw-coloured. With a clear stream flowing gently through the middle, the scene even suggests perfect grasshopper conditions. Only Dale's bulky jacket and the occasional bare willow gives the season away.

Having seen a trout right at the car without even trying, I was expecting a productive session; however, I slowly discovered all was not as it seemed. We continued to sight trout here and there, but most were motionless on the streambed, the barest flicker of their tails the only indication they were alive. Occasionally, in the slowest, sunniest pools, we found a trout hovering just under the surface, sipping the odd midge that had been persuaded to emerge by a hint of late morning warmth. Even these fish were moving in a laboured, almost clumsy way, as if the water was actually thick, clear oil.

On one shaded pool I noticed ice glazing the edge, and curious for an exact reading of what was obviously pretty cold water, I took out my thermometer and dipped it in the river. It read just 3°C, making it the equal coldest water I've knowingly fished. I was surprised by such a low measurement. I'd fished lakes and rivers under heavy snow or searing frost, but hardly ever measured anything under 5°C — at least, not where I was actually casting the fly. I took the temperature again and confirmed it. I could only assume that the Victoria's small size, combined with continuous frosts and snowmelt in its headwaters from the recent blizzard, had created this unlikely anomaly.

Around the next bend the river left the shadows and looked something like inviting water once again. On the edge of a shallow gravelly run, I could make out the shape of a trout, a brown of a pound or so. It seemed fused to the bottom and it was unlikely such a dormant trout would move for a fly, let alone a dry. However, the water looked only centimetres deep and for some reason I decided to cover the fish with a Red Tag dry. The first two casts were completely ignored. I stubbornly presented a third time, and there was a quiver in the trout's body as the fly approached. The fish drifted back sluggishly with the Red Tag, almost nosing it. Then, in a gesture that looked more like a yawn than a take, it opened its mouth wide and the fly sunk down. I waited a second or two and lifted gently. The trout was fat and healthy, the sort of fish that, over summer on the Victoria, often has me in the snags before I've finished lifting the rod. But in water colder than a refrigerator, this one just wriggled on the line like an old, worn-out slab. In the few moments it took to remove the fly from the fish's mouth and return it to the water, my fingers were stinging. When Dale caught up with me several minutes later, I still had my hands in my pockets, trying to thaw them out.

Having caught trout on a fly in rivers and lakes ranging from 3°C to 25°C, water temperature has become another one of those flyfishing factors where the comfortable rules and certainties that appeared to apply in the beginning have seeped away with experience. Even so, I still measure water temperature every time I go fishing. The readings are often important; it's just that the water temperature equation has proven a little more complex than 'can't catch 'em if it's over 20 degrees mate' (or under 6°C for that matter).

What seems to be especially pertinent is *relative* water temperature; that is, the temperature compared to what it's been for the last few hours, last few days or last few weeks. To the short term first, and a rising water temperature is preferable if you can get it. Trout are cold blooded, so if the water is warming, their metabolic rate — all other things being equal — is increasing. More active, hungry trout are likely to be easier to catch. Of course, there's an upper limit to this due to the stresses applied by water that's *too* warm; although, as we've seen, the benefits of warming water can continue beyond supposedly dangerous maximums if the trout have acclimatised first.

Which brings us back to the influence of longer-term temperatures. Remember that diary entry from the Indi that I referred to a few pages back? *'Best day, temp. ranged from 21–23.5°C, yet fishing got better as water got warmer.'* To repeat the point, trout gradually acclimatised to heat over weeks or even months can behave normally in water usually regarded as approaching lethal temperatures, and survive spikes of heat much higher than trout are supposed to be able to tolerate.

Relative temperature is important in terms of place as well as time. Water temperatures are seldom uniform across a given area of trout water. As I mentioned a few pages ago, lakes will often have layers of water of different temperatures, providing cooler water in summer and, less obviously, insulated warmer water in winter. Currents generated by wind or inflowing and outflowing streams can mix some of this water through to the surface, with obvious connotations for trout fishing.

A few Septembers ago I went looking for tailing trout in Tasmania's Lake Kay. This shallow stillwater is one of the fabled Western Lakes and it lies at over 1100 metres above sea level. The car thermometer read −7°C as I began the drive out from Miena on the bumpy road towards the lake and my decision to go fishing was looking dubious. The roadside puddles were frozen solid and some of the smaller lakes were covered in a layer of ice.

By the time I'd walked the last few hundred metres from the car to Lake Kay, the sun was high enough to offer at least a little warmth and the hoarfrost on the grass was melting. The lake margins were still rimmed in ice, however, despite a steady breeze that was generating a good ripple. My initial water temperature reading came out at just 3°C, and even with increasing sunlight offering reasonable visibility into the knee-deep water, there wasn't a sign of a trout, not even one lying 'doggo'. As I walked the margins I checked the temperature regularly, but it remained unchanged. Then I arrived at a bay perfectly aligned with the lee shore and immediately I imagined the water felt slightly less frigid. I checked the thermometer: 6°C. I waded a few more metres: 6°C again. I barely had time to put the thermometer away when a good brown suddenly appeared from behind the nearest tussock. A quick flick of the rod landed my black Woolly Bugger the required three rod lengths away, I held my breath, and the trout swam over and ate it confidently. The fish took off the instant I set the hook and it was all I could do to keep it from heading out of the bay and making a sharp left turn into the deep water and undercuts where I couldn't follow. It was another five minutes before I could slide the net under a 5-pound male brown trout, a fish with that lovely yellowy-gold hue so typical of the Western Lakes.

Over the next hour I caught another slightly smaller trout from the same bay, lost another and spooked two more. Assuming I'd had the best of it, I waded into the next bay, but saw nothing for the next 30 minutes. I checked the water temperature — just 4°C this time. The clock was ticking so I sloshed my way back to the productive bay hoping for another shot. Soon after I stepped out into the open water, I saw a good fish coming along the edge of the tussocks, mouth opening and closing busily. I cast a little short, but the trout rushed over anyway, wolfed down the fly (or appeared to) and I struck confidently. My fly flew over my shoulder without any resistance, and the trout flew out into the bay. Oh well. And yes, the temperature was still 6°C.

That session at Lake Kay neatly demonstrates a key point: when temperatures are at the extreme end, trout will seek more comfortable water; or, at the very least, that's where the active, catchable trout are likely to be. I stress that the *relative* temperature was the important thing that morning at Lake Kay: 6°C is still much colder than ideal, but compared to the 3°C or 4°C alternatives, it created a hot spot, literally and figuratively.

The same rationale applies at the top end of the temperature range. Trout in water that's uncomfortably warm will seek out springs, cool tributaries and other thermal refuges even if the temperature is only a few degrees lower. One stinking hot February day on a tributary of the Mitta Mitta River I caught one of the largest stream trout I've encountered in the area. At 22°C, this stream was only a few degrees cooler than the main river. However, it was attractive enough for a 5-pound Mitta brown (distinctively larger than any of the stream's resident fish) to make its way up from the river junction a couple of hundred metres downstream, where it was feeding aggressively in a small pool. Once again, it was the relative temperature between two nearby spots, not so much the temperature per se, which mattered.

A thermometer, regularly used, will help identify these and countless other opportunities that might otherwise be missed. And in the longer term, recording water temperature, particularly temperature trends on specific waters, will reveal other patterns that are useful. You may find, for example, that local temperature changes influence insect hatches and trout migration. They may encourage (or discourage) certain feeding behaviours, such as tailing in shallow margins.

To summarise, water temperature is undoubtedly an important factor in trout behaviour and therefore catching trout on a fly. However, those who like tidy tables and parameters won't find them here — regional differences, acclimatisation and other variables mean any attempts to be definitive are more misleading than helpful. I keep using the word 'relative' (sorry if it's becoming repetitive) but this really is the key to understanding water temperature and trout.

It is true that if water temperatures are within an ideal range — let's say in the teens (as may often be the case in autumn and spring) — over time and space, temperature may have little obvious impact on the fishing. But make it a habit anyway to measure water temperature often, while being particularly aware of what it might have been in the same place in the recent past, even if you have to make an educated guess. Also compare the water temperature in different locations nearby. Use the information, and you will catch more trout.

BAROMETER AND MOON

THE EXTERNAL VARIABLES that impact on any flyfishing trip can roughly be divided into two groups: those you have some control over and those you don't. I say this on the assumption that most of us are obliged to fish at a pre-arranged time in a pre-arranged area. It's true that if you are lucky enough to live, say, an hour or so from trout water, then there will be occasions when you can spontaneously head off fishing for an evening or an afternoon. In these rare cases you can arguably pick your conditions. Or rather, the circumstances that create the opening are random, but knowing the fishing conditions are right means you can choose to capitalise on the unexpected break. Your late afternoon appointment just called to cancel, the nearest stream has settled and cleared since the last rain and it looks like being a balmy, windless evening.

Mostly though, trips of any substance require some planning, and therefore at least some decisions need to be made in advance about destination, dates, getting there and accommodation. Where possible I will delay a final call about where I'm going until recent conditions and forecasts can be factored in. Even then there comes a point a few days out when you usually must commit to an area, if not a precise river or lake.

On trips like this, barometric pressure is one element that's nearly impossible to plan for or avoid. High and low pressure systems operate on a scale of hundreds, even thousands, of kilometres. Moreover, despite the increasing sophistication of computer models, you can't get an *exact* picture of what these systems will be doing more than a few hours out.

From a given base on a given day, it might be possible to drive from cloudy skies to sunny, from floods to low water, and from hot to cold. However, due to the scale of pressure systems, it is nearly impossible to travel to the barometric pressure you want without getting on a plane. Basically, if you strike changes in air pressure you don't like on a fishing trip, the only way to avoid them is not to fish — a pretty drastic course of action.

Changes in barometric pressure are the subject of much discussion among flyfishers. They're often mentioned as another possible explanation for changes in trout behaviour when, outwardly, little else appears to have altered. Given that barometric pressure is a variable we effectively have no control over except for deciding to fish or not to fish, it's fortunate it has little relevance to trout fishing.

Many fisheries scientists I've talked to are sceptical that trout (as opposed to bottom-dwelling species) even have the ability to detect changes in barometric pressure, let alone respond. Part of their reasoning is that the variation in 'weight' of air on the water is puny compared to the weight of water itself, which is 800 times denser than air. For example, a trout rising up to take a dry fly in just a metre of water will experience a pressure change equivalent to the entire potential range of barometric pressure experienced above the surface — from the most cyclonic depressions to the most stable high pressure systems. For fish, even a decent chop on a lake will produce the equivalent of a dramatic rise and fall in the barometer beneath the surface every time a wave passes overhead.

Leaving aside the hard science, as an avid weather-watcher I can tell you I've had very good trout fishing under every kind of barometric pressure: rising fast, falling fast, low and stable, high and stable, you name it. For that matter, I've had really bad fishing under all sorts of barometric pressure too!

In light of all this, it may come as a surprise that I don't reject barometric pressure entirely as an influence on trout fishing. At the very least, I have no doubt that barometric pressure changes can be detected by, and influence, some of the terrestrial food that trout eat. For example, ants and termites (the trout equivalents of chocolate and crayfish) undergo mass winged migrations that appear to be driven at least in part by pre-thunderstorm plunges in the barometer. (I imagine this is because the migrants need rain-softened soil to make it easier to dig and create a new colony, but don't quote me.)

Another point is that while it might be a stretch for trout to detect actual changes in barometric pressure through the water, it's certain they can detect inputs *related to* barometric pressure changes, such as the rumble of thunder, the flash of lightning, sharp changes in air temperature impacting on the water surface, the effect of wind and wind direction on the surface, the colour and brightness of the sky, precipitation and so on.

Some competent flyfishers remain convinced that the barometer alone is an important influence on fishing success. I'm clearly not one of them; however, I will concede there are times when the behaviour of the trout isn't readily explained by the inputs we can observe. I'm thinking especially of those occasions when the conditions are apparently 'par' yet the trout are uncommonly aggressive or despondent. At these times I do wonder about those hourly changes to the environment around me that I might be oblivious to. I realise that, despite the thousands of days I've spent in the outdoors, I am after all a mere modern human with senses deadened by a life that's not immediately made or broken by the nuances in the natural world. Maybe the closest I can come to experiencing life as a hunter–gatherer 10,000 years ago are those rare occasions when I sense, without conscious effort, that the fishing will be very good (or bad), without a concrete reason.

There are those days when I walk off the water with my friends, pleasantly confused about why the fishing was so productive. We've been known to joke about the alignment of the planets, lucky hats, and similarly pagan explanations. But beneath the frivolity there's an underlying sense that, for all the science and technology at our disposal, there are things about trout and flyfishing we may never understand.

Mentioning planets reminds me that I should offer brief coverage to the moon, another slightly mystical force that seems to divide flyfishers into believers and non-believers. I have friends who plan their fishing lives around moon phase, and I have other friends who wouldn't be able to tell you the current state of the moon if you promised them a ticket to Tasmania. The moon has a potential influence on flyfishing in at least two ways: tidal pull and light. In the ocean, there's no question that tide, and therefore moon phase, can be very important to success. Many of the best saltwater flyfishing charter operations recommend certain slots based on tide: unlike a lot of other variables, tide is one factor that can be planned for months or even years in advance.

Tide can have an influence on sea-trout fishing, albeit a less than straightforward influence depending on location, amount of fresh and so on. Nevertheless, prudent sea-trout fishers are at least aware of what the tide is going to do.

On inland water bodies the effect of the moon is much less clear. Some proponents of moon-phase-based fishing basically argue that the 'pull' of the moon, while tiny compared to its effect on the sea, is still detectable and significant to fish. Personally, I've been unable to observe a meaningful pattern here.

One moon-related factor that is worth mentioning is the effect of a full moon on the quality of dawn fishing for tailers and other trout feeding in the shallows. It seems that the period of soft light before sunrise — dull enough for the trout to feel secure, light enough to locate food — is 'stretched' by a full moon overnight to the point that there's less impetus for inshore trout activity to peak at dawn.

I do have preferences when it comes to night fishing and the light of the moon. To put it simply, I dislike fishing under bright moonlight. The trout seem skittish and what might be described as 'the night fishing factor', when big trout recklessly hit big flies, is usually lost. As if to emphasise the point, thick cloud moving across a bright moon almost always increases the action. So it was on one generally difficult trip to Lake Eucumbene in May. This time of year can produce excellent night fishing as trout gather in Eucumbene's bays and inlets adjacent to the stream mouths, awaiting the right circumstances to begin their spawning run. But exactly *where* the trout wait has a substantial impact on flyfishing success. On this occasion we were dismayed to learn from the trollers that the trout were waiting all right, but in 20 to 30 metres of water, far beyond the reach of any flyfishing equipment.

The trip was saved from virtual ruin on the last evening. In a secluded cove, conveniently not more than a few metres deep, we finally found accessible trout. On a typically frigid Eucumbene night, banks of cloud blew across the moon spasmodically. When the moon was covered, the trout began swirling on the darkened surface within seconds, and our Craigs Nighttime flies were hit as soon as a fish saw them. A lean trip was rapidly transformed as we landed several browns and rainbows to 2 kilograms in the space of a couple of hours. But what I remember as vividly as catching fish again after days of nothing was the extraordinary impact of the moonlight. Moon out, no fish; moon hidden, fish galore. It was as if a giant switch was being flicked on and off.

The same contrast can be found wherever moon shadow falls on the water. Cast a fly into the shade of that big old red gum or cliff face, and the trout behave like nocturnal trout should. They become aggressive predators with little or no room left in their small brains for the caution that can dominate in daylight. Heaven help any mouse, cricket or lizard which finds itself on the water. But right next door, out in the light of the baleful moon, they're as timid as the mice they'd happily eat whole in the shadows. Now the trout cautiously inspect and then refuse innocuous little dry flies, or spook at the flash of a landing fly line.

Of course, as you would expect by this point in the book, there are the exceptions: big falls of moths or crickets under a bright moon, for example, when the mass of easy food temporarily overrides the trout's caution, as does masses of food in most trout fishing situations. But given a choice, I'll take a low moon, covered moon, quarter moon or no moon every time. It may be harder to find your way around, but it's easier to fool a fish.

LIGHT

EVEN IN ITS upper reaches, the South Island's Buller River can be a dauntingly big river. It flows out of the gorgeous Lake Rotoiti in the Nelson Lakes district to then be progressively joined by a number of tributaries that are highly regarded trout rivers in their own right. Eventually it becomes an intimidating giant, only comfortable to flyfish during the lowest of summer flows.

Where Ian and I planned to fish the Buller, some distance below the Gowan River junction, it is still far enough upstream to look like a conventional trout stream with pools, runs and riffles, albeit a big trout stream. We were there in late October after a period of no rain. The exceptionally clear water with only the faintest tinge of blue made the river seem fordable in spots, though once you were halfway across it became apparent that last bit was way too deep and fast to ford except perhaps on the back of a large truck.

I'd timed our run to the river to coincide with the evening rise.

Earlier in the day I'd chatted with the local farmer, who'd been only too happy to permit us to drive down one of his tracks right to a gravel bar beside a particularly promising pool. The beech-forest-clad ridges rose steeply above the thick pasture of the river flats, and although the days were lengthening more than halfway through spring, it was barely after 7 p.m. when the sun was lost somewhere behind the mountain to our west and a long twilight began. However, there was no great rush to the water. We set up our gear carefully on the gravel bar. Tippets and flies were replaced and retied, knots tested. The Buller is no place for a weak link. I kept one eye on the long tapering pool above, but from past experience I knew the rise we'd come for was still most likely some time off.

Soon I'd rigged up with a Kossie Dun (that large white-mast parachute pattern ideal for low-light visibility) and a little tungsten Pheasant Tail Nymph about a metre below. I left Ian the pool above the car, which had produced well on previous trips, and headed several hundred metres upstream and around the bend to a series of runs and riffles. Before I departed, I offered Ian some suggestions (it was his first time on the Buller), including advising that the real action might start quite late. Maybe I should have been a bit more specific.

Despite its clarity, the Buller can be a very difficult river to sight fish. Perhaps it's the mottled colour of the river rocks or the almost transparently pale colouration of the local brown trout, but even under bright sun, you miss spotting a lot of fish. Although it was now early twilight, the way the dark forest backdrop removed all glare from the water made it seem as if I might still be able to sight at least a trout or two, but I couldn't. Never mind; fishing blind I was able to persuade a pair of acrobatic 3-pounders to take the nymph. These browns were sitting right under the inside seam of a crescent-shaped run, within 10 metres of each other. They filled the time nicely until the first duns appeared at 7.45 p.m.

On other Buller evenings I'd noticed a gap between the appearance of the duns and the first rises; even so, I couldn't help feeling anxious once again as I watched the dun numbers explode with absolutely no response from the trout, not visibly anyway. I had to assume that for the moment, the ascending nymphs were a more attractive option to the fish than the emerged duns. Hopefully things would change.

At 8 p.m. they did. In the space of seconds, multiple trout began rising. I might have marvelled for a moment at the synchronicity, but if I did the thought was quickly lost as I realised the trout rising closest to me was a big one. I clipped off the nymph and presented the Kossie Dun on its own. The fly's drift seemed perfect, but at the crucial moment the trout swung off line to eat a real dun. I lifted off and re-presented in a single motion. The Kossie drifted for a foot before a big head engulfed it. The trout moved across the powerful current then did the sensible thing (for a fish) and headed downstream. It took me ten minutes of winding, running and winding again before I beached a long, big-headed Buller brown. It didn't quite match the condition of the first two trout, but it wasn't a slab either at around 5 pounds.

In the time taken to land the trout, check my tippet and dry the fly, the light had become too low to see well over the broken water. Although I could still half hear, half see a few rises, I decided to head back to the pool beside the car. The water was smoother down there, and I would be looking west into the reflected afterglow.

As I rounded the bend and arrived at the top of the pool, I was surprised not to see Ian. Had he headed downstream? I didn't wonder for long, because immediately I could identify at least half a dozen fish, rising hard where the elongated triangle shape of the pool broadened about midway to the tail. The light was fading by the minute, but because the middle of the pool was smooth and there was some light reflected from the west, I could see the rises quite clearly. It wasn't so easy to see the pale mast of the Kossie. The main feeding lane, where the bubble line pulsed and twisted was roughly halfway across the pool; a good 15 metres away. I strained to see the fly as it drifted into the minefield of rises … think that was me … strike! Err, no. My fly skated off the water about a metre above where the real rise occurred.

The next cast was virtually a repeat, only this time I managed to stay locked onto the tiny white dot that indicated my fly. The Kossie drifted into the vicinity of two trout rising hard side-by-side, and then it was gone in a boisterous take. I went to lift but the bowing line had already set the hook and the trout was blasting towards the far bank. I very nearly snapped it off, only dropping the tip and letting the line slip in the nick of time. I then recovered to lift the rod upright as the trout leapt noisily in the shadow of the steep slope opposite. My fly line was nearly gone, but fortunately at that point the fish chose not to bolt down with the flow, but to head for some real or imagined refuge upstream. Slowly it bored up into the current, and slowly I winched it towards my bank. As I steered the trout into the shallows adjacent to the gravel bar where I stood, it gave one last lunge, this time downstream. However, the fish was too far from the main current now. It wasn't difficult to throw it off balance with a sideways rod and at last it was on the edge of the gravel. The trout was 4 pounds of absolutely prime Buller muscle, almost as unyielding to the touch as the wet river rocks on which it lay. I removed the fly and gently held the fish upright in the water, wanting to give it time to re-orientate itself. But in an instant it gave a powerful kick and dashed out into the river, leaving a plume of whitewater behind it.

I stood up and blew the fly dry, briefly checking it with my headlamp. Out in the river one or two fish rose sporadically still, their disturbances just visible as faint drifting rings through the faint remaining patch of afterglow. It was 8.30 p.m. and I half-heartedly thought about casting again when I heard the car door open about 100 metres downstream. 'That you, Phil?' called Ian.

'Yep,' I answered, turning and walking towards him, 'How did you go?'

'No good,' came the reply in the dark.

I waited until I was back at the car before continuing the conversation. As I began removing my wading boots, Ian sipped contentedly on a cup of thermos coffee. 'So not much happened downstream?' I asked.

'Don't know,' Ian responded, 'I stuck it out here. Quite a few duns drifted down about quarter to eight, but nothing took 'em.' He had another sip of coffee while I struggled with the left leg of my waders, which seemed to have welded to my foot. 'So it was getting dark by then and I headed back here.'

I thought about a nice way to break it to Ian that he'd missed out on some really good fishing through finishing too early, but nothing came to mind so I just told him the truth. 'Hate to say it, mate,' I began, 'but the trout got up on the duns really well — only it took them a little while to get started.'

'Not down here,' Ian insisted, but then I explained how my first fish took the fly around 8 p.m., and that the rise was in full swing when I arrived at 'his' pool ten or so minutes later. 'Didn't really slow down until 8.30,' I continued, 'And I'll bet it was going here at least by 8, maybe even a few minutes earlier in this flatter water.'

On the drive back out, we talked about evening rises. Although Ian confessed he found it hard fishing in the poor light, I did my best to persuade him how productive that last relic of daylight can be for fishing. I also explained some of the tricks that can be used to overcome the encroaching darkness, like using the afterglow in the west, or striking on a hunch (even if your hunch isn't always right) and putting on your headlamp early so it's immediately convenient for checking flies and leaders.

Ian eventually gave in and agreed to stay on the water until 8.30 p.m. the next evening. We headed back to the same stretch of the Buller, and although the rise wasn't quite as intense as the evening before, he caught a 4-pounder right on 8.15 p.m.

On lakes, change of light — the transition from day to night or vice versa — is the most reliable time to catch a trout on a fly. On rivers, I'd moderate that statement somewhat to say evening is certainly the most reliable time (all other things being equal) while dawn *can* be good, depending on factors which we'll look at shortly.

For trout, change of light is a time when their senses are particularly capable in terms of seeking food. Their superb eyesight and ability to detect sounds and vibrations give them an edge when the light is low. At the same time, the fish become instinctively aware that it's more difficult for their own predators to locate and catch them, so they become less cautious. To top it all off, many of the bugs trout eat choose change of light as the least dangerous time to migrate, emerge or procreate, thus providing a spike in available food. This is especially evident on lakes. On rivers, evening remains a premium time for insect activity. Dawn activity, although sometimes significant, is more likely to be moderated by the cool temperatures that prevail at daybreak. It's no surprise then that the best dawn hatches on streams tend to occur during generally hot weather.

Overall I do think the precious hour or so at the beginning of the day (lakes) and at the end (rivers and lakes) tends to be underutilised by flyfishers. I'm as guilty as anyone when it comes to dawn. Not being a morning person, the effort to actually be on the water and ready to fish at the first hint of light often defeats me. And I'm only too aware that being there late means I might as well not be there at all. Or at least, I may have some reasonable fishing, but the change of light advantage is lost.

I make amends on evening though, having been convinced long ago of the value of staying around until the very last light is gone (by which I mean it's dark enough to see the first stars) and sometimes beyond. Evening on lakes or streams falls short of coming with a guarantee of good fishing, but not by much. So long as water conditions are within the broad realm of reasonable and the weather conditions stay this side of despicable, the trout are likely to feed more visibly and be more catchable than usual. That should be reason enough to stay on, but those who commit often will also encounter exceptional sport with pleasing frequency — evenings when the fishing is so good that you'll have to go back and check your fishing diary a few months later just to make sure you didn't dream it.

Although dawn and dusk are the tidiest examples when it comes to discussions about light (low light in this context being nearly always a good thing), light — or lack of it — continues to affect trout and flyfishing opportunities throughout the 24-hour cycle. We've already covered moonlight; during daylight the angle of the sun and presence or absence of cloud can all have an influence on flyfishing. The most obvious impact of sunlight on the water relates not so much to the fish, but how easy they are to see. When searching for trout with polarised glasses, a high sun and little or no cloud is what's generally hoped for. On many New Zealand rivers, where sight fishing is not just a nice little bonus but pretty much essential to success, sunlit water is a must. On streams flowing through broad valleys with little bankside vegetation, sunlight limited by cloud or angle makes spotting trout very difficult — and spotting trout before casting is all but essential on those rivers where the trout are big but numbers are low.

The same applies to many lake fisheries, such as Tasmania's Western Lakes or the Great Lake. Without good sun, the broad-scale searching you rely on to locate a target becomes nearly impossible. If you're lucky, rises or other disturbances may give the fish away, but generally on the open clearwaters — river or lake — where sight fishing is so important, no sun means no fun.

Things are not so sunshine-reliant where sight fishing locations have a substantial backdrop of bush, cliff or mountainside. Early in my Tasmanian fishing I was relieved to discover that, even if I lost the sun, by wading out and facing back towards steep or forested shores, I could maintain a window into the trout world. Years later when I was first guided in New Zealand by Craig Simpson, I was surprised when he chose the apparently dim light of a forested gorge stream on the basis it was cloudy. The surprise only lasted for about a minute after we pushed through the dark beech forest to the water's edge, which was how long it took Craig to spot the 6-pounder finning attentively beneath the bubble line in front of us. It was so easy to see, even I could spot it. The flat light in the gorge actually made it simpler to look into the water; without shadows cast by the sun, there was nowhere we couldn't see. (Craig commented later that he couldn't see very well into shadow and so avoided this particular spot on sunny days — a sobering statement from a man who seems to have some sort of infrared vision.)

Basically, white reflected light is the enemy when polaroiding. If you can replace white reflections with dark ones, then you can see into the water. You can also reduce the problems of limited sunlight and/or white reflections by gaining height above the water. The more you're looking straight down on the water, the better your ability to penetrate the depths and the less reflected light. This is one reason it's so easy to spot fish from bridges — great fun with a friend, but not so great when you're on your own and you climb back down to water level. Now exactly where was that fish again? In front of the second pylon or the third?

Besides its impact on our ability to see fish, light is significant in the lifecycle of some important trout water insects. We've already looked at the boom in insect activity around the beginning and especially the end of the day. Beyond that, mayfly emergences are often related to daytime light intensity. There are stark differences between regions and species, but these are worth becoming familiar with. For example, daytime mayfly hatches on some New Zealand rivers are favoured by bright sunshine, in contrast to the hatches on the lakes around my central Victorian home, which are at their best on cloudy days.

Of course, trout behaviour is itself influenced by light. I've already mentioned that trout undoubtedly feel more secure when they sense they are less visible to predators. At the same time, trout appear to see better without the intensity of full sunlight. Trout leaping for flying dragonflies, damselflies and spinners are always more active when the sun goes behind the cloud. Catching fast-moving insects midair requires perfect vision, and on many lakes I fish, on partly cloudy days it's as if the trout are jumping jacks, ignited by cloud and snuffed out by sun.

Before we leave the topic of light, I should touch on the related subject of fog. Given the preceding comments, it might be assumed that fog and the diffused light that goes with it would help flyfishing. In fact, I find it a negative. On rivers, the descent of fog seems to kill off most activity, stifling hatches and falls. Even subsurface activity appears to be subdued by its cold breath. On lakes, trout can continue to feed in the fog quite well, but far from helping to conceal the angler, it seems to highlight us. Rods, lines and particularly boats, arms and bodies are silhouetted more boldly than on the brightest days. Even the most careful flyfisher tends to loom up out of the uniformly pale backdrop of fog looking like Bigfoot — and the trout tend to respond accordingly. I'm not saying you can't fish in the fog, just that I'd prefer not to.

ON THE LEVEL

IF I'M EXCHANGING fishing reports with my friends, one element that comes up quickly is the height of the water in question. Too high, too low or just right? If Trevor tells me, as he did just now on the phone, that the Geehi River in the Snowy Mountains is a good height, I know what he means. Just as he would know what I meant if I reported that the Ovens River was a good height.

No further elaboration is required, at least not on that particular point. From Trevor's two-word description, I can picture the Geehi being comfortably wadeable at the pool tails, but with enough current to maintain a drift of food and bubbles through all but the biggest pools. At the same time, there wouldn't be so much flow as to render the riffles and pocket water an unfishable torrent.

I guess if either of us stopped to think about it, we'd summarise 'the right height' — at least in the case of many freestone rivers and tailwaters — as one that balances accessibility with enough flow to keep the fish feeling secure and to help drift our flies in a way that adds to their lifelike appearance. It also doesn't hurt if the flies travel at a pace that denies the trout the chance to look at them too carefully, but not so fast that the fish can't be bothered chasing them down.

I've learnt over the years that simply looking from a distance is not an accurate way of assessing river level. It's surprising how a relatively small difference in height — perhaps the difference between a particular crossing being knee deep or thigh deep — can equate to a major change in current velocity, often a doubling at least.

Overall, the tendency for any trout stream to look 'about right' at first view can be misleading. For one thing, after a few hours on the road the anticipation as you initially glimpse water is likely to colour the view. So despite my familiarity with many streams, I still need to see a reference point to get a sense of what the river height really is. Along the Indi River on the New South Wales border, it's a single large swordgrass tussock visible from the Biggara Road. This tussock has survived more floods than several red gums and at least one bridge. If it's actually sitting in the water, then the river is higher than I like it. If, on the other hand, it forms a small island, it's perfect. On the Mitta Mitta River near Tallandoon I want to see little if any water flowing down an anabranch near one of the wayside stops. Along the Arnold River below Lake Brunner in New Zealand, when I look upstream from the first bridge, I hope to note a small strip of exposed gravel between the willows and the water's edge. (And yes, I know there are useful websites where you can check the latest river heights down to the centimetre, but 'latest' is often still several hours old; more by the time you add travel beyond computer range.)

In each case, observing a level other than what I consider perfect is not a disaster. There are ways of fishing the Arnold when it's up against the willows, or the Mitta when the anabranch is flowing strongly. However, after many trips, I've found that a certain level (give or take a few centimetres) is an extremely promising start. It follows that where I have a choice of several nearby streams, I usually make the effort to find those that are at the right level. A typical trip might be summarised like this: my friends and I arrive in the central south of New Zealand early in the season (spring) to find the main stem rivers like the Ahuriri too high, but the smaller tributaries flowing at that perfect wadeable, coverable and just plain fishable level.

However, later in the season (autumn) when things have dried out, the situation is often reversed. The smaller rivers and creeks become low and difficult, while the larger rivers have dropped to that ideal, manageable height. This sort of pattern is repeated in nearly every trout district on either side of the Tasman. The key point to note is that the very conditions that lead some streams to be too high often make others nearby just right — and vice versa.

Overall, stream height is one of those basic factors in flyfishing — like the simple presence or absence of available food — that can have a very big influence on success. By all means consult solunar tables and barometric pressure graphs, and search the sandbars for suspicious footprints, but it pays not to overlook the importance of how strongly your chosen stream is or isn't flowing.

Not, as I stress again, that high flows are all bad. On freestone rivers and tailwaters, high flows can provide exceptional edge and backwater fishing, while along slower 'meadow' streams, they can create floodwater feeder opportunities as the water spills gently onto nearby flats.

In fact, on some streams I fish, high flows are not merely tolerable but hoped for. For example, while the lowland rivers in western Victoria can provide engrossing fishing during the clear almost flowless conditions of summer and autumn, the same waters are close to their best during high water in spring. We fish big wet flies to large browns that are at their most savage in the swirling, discoloured currents.

Unusually low or dry conditions can also provide opportunities. My best ever session on the South Island's lower Buller River came during a mini-drought. With this very large and dangerously swift river temporarily reduced to something less intimidating, we were able to access a stretch we could never contemplate normally (and haven't been able to reach since!). Wandering a rarely exposed gravel island with the deafening pitch of cicada calls surrounding us on the beech forest slopes, my brother Mark and I could fish big dries and nymphs through two adjacent anabranches. Judging by their aggressive response, I doubt if the 4-pound browns in those anabranches had ever seen a fly.

Overall, stream level is very important and it should always be towards the top of a flyfisher's considerations. But like so many elements of the flyfishing equation, it can't be neatly packaged up and delivered without accounting for the significant exceptions.

Lake levels are every bit as important to flyfishing opportunities as stream levels, as many tales in this book already suggest. However, it's not so much a fixed, hoped for height that tends to preoccupy me when I first glimpse the lake I'm heading to, but rather its *relative* height compared to what it has been. I could make the sweeping generalisation that receding lakes are bad, stable lakes are good, and rising lakes are the best of all, and I guess that's a useful starting point. However, barely have I finished typing the words and the exceptions come flooding in, so to speak.

To rising lake levels first, and let me offer an example. Several years ago I headed to Lake Cairn Curran on a hunch that the stable waters of late winter had begun to rise. Following a dry winter, there had been a period of good rain that had likely boosted the inflowing streams, and outflows were still at pre-irrigation season lows. My hopes appeared to be realised when I drove up to the bay before Picnic Point late in the afternoon and noticed the water lapping into the margin of short grass — grass which had managed to form a green fuzz over the bare earth last covered by water in mid autumn. The rain that had caused the rising water had stopped, but the sky was still a heavy grey and the light was lower than it should have been for the time of day. It was also calm and ideal for spotting fish. In short, the conditions looked perfect.

I rigged up quickly and had hardly finished tying on a small olive Woolly Bugger when I noticed a fin appear on the glassy surface. It was just a rod length out from where the track I was parked on disappeared into the lake. I crept to within a few metres of the water and cast from my knees to just ahead of a second disturbance made by the fish. The plop of the Woolly was acknowledged by a wriggling bow-wave, a pause, and then a big swirl as the trout probably ate it ... Yes! I lifted into resistance and the 3-pound brown went hurtling out into the bay, obviously intent on reaching the sanctuary of deeper water. I worked the fish back quicker than I probably should have, not wanting to overstretch my tippet, but keen to make the most of the light (which was fading with surprising speed) to find other trout. The gentle slope of crew-cut grass was perfect for beaching the fish, its distended belly evidence of the bounty of worms and other bugs that were obviously being flushed by the rising lake.

Racing the light, I found three more trout working the shallows. One I lined when I misjudged its direction — trout feeding hard in low light are fairly forgiving, but even they won't tolerate a fly line landing on their backs! The other two I caught, both around the same size as the first. Barely had I landed the last one when the light evidently dropped a notch too far and the trout could no longer see well enough to harvest the shallows. I couldn't complain though. I'd had an hour of sport for which I would have happily driven much further than 80 kilometres. On my way home through the mist-shrouded hills around Daylesford, I was already planning my return at dawn.

I was almost cackling in triumph as I headed off in the dark the next morning, the starless sky confirming the persistence of the thick blanket of cloud. If a bare hour of fishing had yielded such rewards the evening before, what treats awaited me if I had trout foraging under a whole day of overcast skies?

As the first soft light began to give form to the landscape beyond the headlights, I turned onto the Pyrenees Highway — only

15 kilometres to go. Then I crossed a minor creek and was surprised to notice it was filling its banks almost to bridge level. Strange, I hadn't noticed that yesterday. A few kilometres on, the highway crossed the Joyces Creek arm of Lake Cairn Curran itself. This arm is at the southern extremity of the lake and it had been empty the previous day; now in the first light I could see water spread over the flats below the bridge.

Confused and concerned, I continued on to the bay at Picnic Point. But when I arrived it wasn't there, replaced instead by an unrecognisable sheet of water. I found out later that a big storm had hit the northern slopes of the ranges during the night, sending a massive flood down the Loddon River, Cairn Curran's main feeder. I got out of the car in a daze, after parking about 50 metres back from my spot the day before, which was now somewhere out in the lake.

I robotically took my rod out of the car, still rigged up from the night before, and headed towards the unfamiliar shore. Gone was the neat fringe of young grass; now the newly turbid waters pushed up into waist-high thistles and docks, plants that had grown on the upper lakebed with impunity during the dry seasons that had persisted over the past couple of years. I waded as far as I could but was barely able to reach the open water. I had to cast over the drowning weeds to fish effectively.

It occurred to me that if I hooked a trout, I'd almost certainly lose it in the mess between the open water and my position. However, as I continued to cast and retrieve the fly, I began to accept that this was an unlikely problem, and not just because of the muddy water or flooded clutter. The sudden rise in water would have flushed a phenomenal amount of food from literally hectares of lakebed. The previous afternoon, there had been that reasonably tidy balance between food supply and demand that every flyfisher on a rising lake hopes for. The trout were well fed, but only as long as they foraged at the edge of the creeping tide.

Not any more, however. The trout would still be in the area all right, but spoilt for choice as they rummaged around way out in the lake somewhere, and metres below the surface. There was no need for them to risk the dangers of the shallows now when they could fill their stomachs many times over without ever coming within range of a predator like me.

Not for the first time in my flyfishing life, hope temporarily over-rode reason. I mean, it was less than a day earlier that this spot had fished brilliantly. Surely there must be one or two adventurous, errant trout willing to explore the boundaries of their new kingdom? So I stayed on for another hour, casting and taking the occasional step backwards as the perceptibly rising water kept sneaking towards the top of my waders. But there was not a sign of a trout, not a rise, not a dimple, not the slightest suspicious bump on my line. Eventually I shrugged, waded out of the lake and headed home.

The Picnic Point experience is one that's encountered often in wet years. The trout themselves nearly always thrive in such conditions, and in fact, can quickly reach exceptional size as all that flooded ground causes a boom in the lake's productivity. Indeed, Cairn Curran produced exceptional trout on the fly — fish up to 3 kilograms and more — when things ultimately settled down again after that flood event. But on lakes everywhere the issues are similar when the water rises too fast: no incentive for the trout to feed inshore, and the sheer physical difficulty for the angler in finding open water to fish.

A third issue arises on lakes that have permanent or semi-permanent weedbeds. By definition, such weedbeds tend to establish during periods of relatively stable levels (aquatic weed cannot survive if left high and dry, or when submerged too deep to access sunlight). During such stable periods, flyfishers can reach the trout that haunt these fertile areas relatively easily. But when lake levels rise very quickly, as happened recently at Lake Jindabyne in the Snowy Mountains, the weedbeds are left behind — often many metres down and a long way offshore. This then is one advantage of stable lake levels: they may not provide the boom times offered by rising water, but you can have pretty good, reliable fishing to trout feeding on the various creatures that have settled in and around the aquatic gardens.

Falling lake levels are the least preferred fishing option. I was searching in vain for trout one day along a receding Bronte Lagoon shoreline in Tasmania when the fisheries biologist mate I was with said, in a moment of anthropomorphic weakness, that he thought the trout were absent because they were scared of being stranded. That may have been attributing to the trout more capacity for rational thought than they are capable of, but on an instinctive level it is possible trout know that falling levels, in shallow water at least, are best avoided.

S-l-o-w-l-y receding levels, such as affect many lakes over late summer and autumn, tend not to be such a problem for flyfishing. It seems that aquatic life, trout included, adapts well to a gradual decrease so long as the overall lake level does not become critically low. Receding water can even create opportunities. At Millbrook's Cabin Lake, when the water retreats out of the reeds and shallowest flats in late summer, the resident minnows lose valuable hiding places. Suddenly, the trout, which have ignored the minnows for months, begin targeting them, creating some wonderful smelter fishing.

Come to think of it, I can even conjure up an example when a rapidly falling lake can produce good fishing. My Tasmanian friends Greg and Lindsay have both told me about exciting fishing at Laughing Jack Lagoon. Here the trout ambush water slaters as they are forced off the flats when the lagoon drops to feed the local hydro-electricity scheme.

For all the exceptions though, I think I will go back to the initial generalisation and suggest flyfishers seek slowly rising or stable lakes as their first choice — at least if such lakes are available within striking distance.

FISHING PRESSURE

JIM IS NEVER the most cheerful person, but when he phoned me after his January trip to the Nariel Creek in north-east Victoria, he sounded more morose than usual. 'Cars had squashed the grass at all the bridges, and the banks had footprints everywhere,' he explained sadly, 'It was fished out!'

Hmmm, I silently thought to myself, that doesn't sound right. I knew the Nariel had enjoyed a very good spring and early summer, and I found it hard to believe all the trout I'd encountered before Christmas were gone or uncatchable, notwithstanding the hammering the stream can get over the peak summer holiday period. I pushed Jim for a bit more detail. Through his stories of woeful fishing, a couple of key points gradually emerged. He was only fishing the slow pools because, 'My eyes aren't so good these days and I can't see the fly in the faster water.' Then, discouraged by the lack of action, he was off the water and back at his caravan before sunset.

I tried to think of a nice way to explain to Jim that with these two factors alone he had basically sabotaged the best fishing. But nothing came to mind, so after listening politely and making non-committal comments like 'Is that right?' and 'I see ...', I wished him goodnight.

Anglers are forever looking for reasons for lack of success that are distinct from their own efforts, and fishing pressure (or variations on the theme) is near the top of the heap of reasons given for a bad day's trout fishing. Superficially, this makes sense. Any trout water, let alone a relatively small water like a stream, carries a finite number of fish, and if other anglers have caught or scared those fish before you get there, it can't have helped.

However, as with so many things to do with flyfishing and trout, the consequences of fishing pressure are not so simple that they can be packaged in a box labelled 'Bad' and left at that. Many of the most popular trout waters are, of course, fished very heavily. I've written previously about my experiences on Japan's Yu River, a pretty mountain stream about four hours' drive north of Tokyo. No wider than a single lane road, the accessible stretches often see a flyfisher every 20 metres or so. The local brook trout are undoubtedly aware, in their simple way, that the strange upright things on the river's edge are up to no good. Or more to the point, that insects which aren't really insects and are attached to lines are trying to catch them. Non-fishers (and there are plenty hiking and picnicking along the Yu's banks) are actually ignored by the trout; even among those actively fishing, it's really their lines and flies that are viewed with suspicion more than those casting them.

The trout continue to feed among the incongruous crowd, and although the fishing is certainly challenging, the Yu is still a rewarding place to flyfish — hence the number of fishers! Clever pattern selection, fly-first presentation and perfect drifts will ultimately fool enough trout to keep most anglers happy.

One of the ironies here is that the trout have become habituated to the presence of people precisely because the fishing pressure is so high. Evidently, to a Yu River trout, humans have become part of the scenery just like the trees and rocks. In any case, if the fish were to cease feeding and hide every time a person appeared, they would starve.

At the other extreme, trout which are hardly ever fished to can be ridiculously edgy. One oft-quoted New Zealand study claimed that some big brown trout in a remote backcountry river hid for days after merely sensing anglers, never mind being caught or even fished to unsuccessfully. Such a response is probably best explained as an 'if in doubt, flee' reaction. Exposed to something large, alive and unfamiliar, successful trout are those that instinctively hide, rather than hang around to find out if the potential threat is, in fact, dangerous.

My personal experiences on virgin (or near virgin) waters have been less emphatic, but I've certainly learned that trout which have effectively never seen an angler can be every bit as easy to spook as those on more heavily fished waters. Certainly such trout can be quite naïve about flies and lines, but they are as flighty as any fish in response to sudden movement, a careless footfall or the flash of a shiny rod or wristwatch.

I can give endless examples of fishing pressure having no perceptible impact on fishing quality. On holidays, I often stay on a stretch of a given river or stream for several days, during which time my friends and I fish and re-fish the same water repeatedly. It might be expected that this level of pressure would see a steady decline in fishing quality over the trip, but it never does. My diaries consistently show that numbers of trout caught and average size are likely to be the same at the end of our holiday as at the beginning when the trout were (theoretically!) 'fresh'. It's the usual suspects like water temperature, hatches and variations in stream flow that are far more likely to influence fishing success, not whether or not the water has been fished a lot.

As my understanding of the realities of fishing pressure has developed, it's not surprising that I've become less obsessed with finding lightly fished water. Although I'm fortunate to have formed some great friendships with landowners who just happen to have trout streams flowing through their properties, I'm less inclined than ever to seek out this 'pseudo' private fishing. (While most Australian trout streams are not privately owned, the surrounding land often is, and anglers are required to seek permission before crossing private land to reach a stream.)

Often, when faced with a choice between opening and closing several gates and bumping down a rough, boggy track to the river or simply driving to the next bridge or wayside stop to start fishing, I choose the latter. In short, these days I'm most likely to cross private property to fish because there's a certain type of water there — say a long, even glide or extensive riffle — rather than to escape fishing pressure.

Inevitably, there are exceptions to my generally easy attitude to fishing pressure. Streams with low numbers of trout — large waters or small — are more of a worry to fish secondhand. With few potential targets to begin with, any trout recently caught and kept, caught and released, pricked, or simply frightened some other way, are fish deducted from an already limited budget. Speaking of which, excessive angler take can certainly be a problem too: if a substantial proportion of a water's overall trout population — particularly the better fish — is being removed by anglers, this will cause a very real decline in fishing quality. With many trout waters managed by sensible bag and size limits and closed seasons (and with trout surviving careful release very well) this is less of an issue than it once was. Still, there are a few trout waters I fish where I worry that the angler take is higher than it should be.

The other issue in all this is, of course, the angling experience apart from the actual catching of fish. This element is far more subjective and difficult to measure, but whereas it's often easy to counter claims of 'too many other anglers' spoiling the catch rate, it's not so easy to be dismissive of the all-important happiness factor (for want of a better description!) of which, as any flyfisher knows, the catching is only a part.

Much of this aspect of fishing pressure can be managed by managing expectations. No Japanese angler is likely to be disappointed to find dozens of cars parked by the Yu River trailhead on a fine day. It's expected, and due to a culture that encourages a well-developed sense of personal space, each angler can fish within 10 or 20 metres of the next without any sense of intrusion.

At the other extreme, backcountry New Zealand streams are places where even a single encounter with another angler during a trip can be devastating — at least to some. I've fished with backcountry guides who examine broken twigs and possible footprints like CSI on the trail of a murderer. Such a level of concern about a previous angler visit — even a visit days ago — can be contagious. Regardless of the real impact (or not) on fishing success, the expectation or at least the hope is that a whole river will be the preserve of you and your mates for the duration of your visit. Once you get used to that idea, any encounter with a stranger can become a downer.

Finally, the presence of another angler can have an impact on where you fish, or at least where you feel it's appropriate to fish, even if you don't think the actual trout are being pestered in any meaningful sense. Arriving at a favourite pool or lake corner to find another angler usually means the right thing to do is to go somewhere else. This can mean anything from minor inconvenience to deep disappointment, depending on things like how badly you wanted to have another crack at the fish you saw there last night and how far it is to the next promising spot.

Ultimately, I have a split personality when it comes to fishing pressure. In my heart, I'd rather have anywhere I choose to go fishing entirely to myself and whoever I'm fishing with. I can't help but give a silent cheer when I arrive at the bridge and mine is the only car, or in a prime bay without the ominous upright shape of another angler on the other side. (I've even been known to quietly curse tree stumps in the half light, until I realised they were tree stumps.)

However, in my head, I know that fishing in general, and flyfishing in particular, survives only because of popularity. I don't intend for this book to drift into the politics of fishing, but it's unavoidable at this point to say that there are significant forces, from green fundamentalists to the more extreme animal rights activists, who would dearly like to see fishing of any kind gone. Fishing will survive while it remains popular, and the price of popularity is that we may sometimes need to share fishing more than we would, on a primitive level at least, like to.

STRIKING

HAVING LINED UP all the components leading to that thrilling moment when a trout actually eats your fly, there are still a few more crucial steps to take before your fish is safely in the net. The first of these is striking or, to remove any sense of violence from the action, let's say 'setting the hook'. The window of opportunity to set the hook in flyfishing is very narrow for the simple but fundamental reason that artificial flies taste bad. Yes, the good ones are clever visual frauds; however, even the most exquisite mayfly or minnow imitation still tastes like fur and metal garnished with a dob or two of petroleum by-product and a dash of toxic glue. Within a moment of tasting flies, fish very sensibly spit them out.

So it is that flyfishers face a unique problem when it comes to hooking fish. Strike too soon and the fish hasn't got the fly properly in its mouth; strike too late and it's already being ejected like a lemon pip in a cocktail. The difference can sometimes be measured in nanoseconds.

Besides timing, there's the nature of the strike. Lift the rod or strip-strike? Firm or gentle? The opportunities for error are endless.

There are ways of improving your strike, but first most of us need to accept that, as with dancing in public, how we *think* we strike and how we *actually* strike are two different things. One late summer day, a well-known flyfisher and I were casting to rises on the edge of a Tasmanian lake. A large brown sucked down my Red Tag, and I struck with what I imagined was the poise of a gymnast and the timing of an elite golfer. The hook briefly bit then flew speedily past my cheek. 'You trying to snap his nostrils off?' my friend gasped through peals of laughter.

'I thought I lifted at about the right moment,' I replied defensively, but doubt was creeping in.

As luck would have it, I was videoing my mate half an hour later when he too had a rise. The strike was so violent that if it had connected something would have broken. However, careful analysis of the tape later showed there was no chance of this because my friend struck before the trout had actually eaten his fly. Back at our lodgings that evening I endlessly replayed the moment. Forward, backward, frame by frame. It was fascinating. Well, I thought so.

That day, both my companion and I were reminded of a major obstacle to striking correctly: the general inability to override an instinctive or emotional reaction. And herein lies the Catch 22: during one of flyfishing's most thrilling moments, ideally you should behave as coolly as a well-programmed robot. For example, 'slow take, slow strike' is one useful tip when dry-fly fishing. 'Wait until he turns back down,' advises one venerable gentleman, only to be surpassed by another steel-nerved soul who insists, 'Wait until he turns back down and the leader starts to move, *then* strike.' Fine, but in the slow-motion world surrounding a rise to a dry fly, where heartbeats are several seconds apart, the latter example could mean delaying the strike for about half an hour.

There are a few ways the speedy dry-fly strikers among us can slow things down. One is to actually put the rod on the grass or gravel after casting. Another (although you can't plan for it) is to receive a slow rise to your fly while, say, applying sunscreen or admiring an eagle overhead. The resulting strike will have all the elegance of walking backwards into the paint stand at the hardware, but at least it will be delayed. One of my fishing mates who's a confessed premature striker shakes his polaroids off when it looks like a fish is going to notice his dry fly. He says, that way, at least he won't see the take until the trout's nose breaks the water, and won't be tempted to strike any earlier. Now there is a man who knows his limitations.

Guides are never happy with your strike, and I speak with the authority of one who is both guide and guided. I'm sure it would bring tears of quiet joy to many of my clients if they could watch me having a bad day under the exasperated gaze of Kiwi guide Craig Simpson. Never a more cheerful or patient guide will you meet, but I don't think I've ever struck a nymphing trout quite to Craig's satisfaction. When I do hook one, there's usually an exclamation of mild surprise from Craig, along the unstated lines of 'I'll be buggered, you hooked 'im despite your slow/fast/violent/too soft strike.'

When guid*ing*, you get to observe from the safe and superior position of not having a rod in your hand. In light of the above paragraph, any criticisms I'm about to make may seem a tad hypocritical. Still, I do see some breathtaking efforts. The too fast strike I can relate to, the too slow strike I can accept, but an utter failure to strike at all does call for some deep breathing and a silent count to ten. There was a time when I occasionally had to take some responsibility for the non-strike, having rushed a few beginners to the water without any explanation of this crucial step. 'Strike, strike!' I'd scream, as a good trout miraculously sucked down their fly (despite it being cast too short or inaccurately), only to receive a puzzled look from my inanimate charge. 'What's a strike?'

Believe me, this only has to occur a handful of times and you begin preaching striking like the born again. These days, before my class is even allowed near the water they've practised striking on the grass, memorised diagrams and repeated after me 'Flies taste bad'.

Of course, having graduated from Striking 101, there is no telling where their fish-hooking careers may lead. Some years after his first lesson, I guided Ed on a day when the grasshopper feeders were proving inexplicably difficult to hook. The fish would appear to take the fly well, but Ed's considered strikes were barely feeling resistance. 'Try counting to four,' I suggested, conveniently overlooking the fact I would struggle to do this myself. A large trout came up and chomped down his foam hopper. Ed counted, 'One ... two ...'

'YEP!' I yelled.

He glanced at me quizzically, then quietly said, 'Three ... four.' His rod came up, and immediately bent under the weight of a 3-pound brown, hooked firmly in the jaw scissors. I slipped the net under the fish a few minutes later, and Ed said, 'Guess you count faster than me.'

Dry-fly fishing is almost always about reacting to *the sight* of your fly being eaten, and it's this fact which makes it possible (as we have seen) to respond too quickly as well as too slowly. With wet-fly fishing, problems setting the hook can mostly be narrowed down to the latter: you are usually responding to cues *after* the fly has been taken, because it is difficult to impossible to watch the trout actually eat a submerged fly. At best, a wet-fly fisher presenting their artificial in very clear water may watch for a response from a sighted trout and make a judgement about when to lift the rod, based on, say, the white 'wink' of a mouth opening and closing, or the deliberate movement of a trout to where the fly should be. Even then, the uncertainty creates a built-in delay.

Now I don't want to discourage anyone in a sight-fishing situation from striking on the basis of visual cues from the trout. This is a great skill to develop and will catch you fish when other cues, like moving indicators or lines, fail — more on this shortly. More often than not though, a wet-fly fisher has no visual contact with the trout at all. It's only through movement of the line, leader or strike indicator that the angler is aware a fish may have taken the fly. This is when a hair-trigger reaction is something to aim for. By the time a take is transmitted, things have already happened beneath the water and out of sight.

The delay between a take and some physical clue to this can be considerable. Recently I was guiding a relatively experienced angler, Doug, when, despite the glary white cloud in the sky above, we spotted a huge trout cruising the shallow flat in front of us. I first sighted the big brown moving away to the right, following the line of an old pump pipe. Cruising brown trout especially seem to like the presence of some sort of structure — logs, ledges, weedbeds and so on. Whether such structure is used to maintain bearings, to help hide the fish or both, I'm not sure. In this case, the inch-wide strip of old black poly pipe offered no meaningful cover for the fish, but it followed it religiously until the pipe ran out and the trout disappeared. I silently questioned my decision to suggest Doug delay casting. Casting after a departing trout is risky in the extreme, with even the most accurate cast likely to line the fish. Still, as the seconds ticked by and the monster failed to reappear, I'm sure Doug was wondering if he'd missed a very rare chance.

Then I spotted the fish again. It must have swum out wide and circled back, so it was coming along the pipe once more, only this time well to our left, moving right and towards us. It was a good 10 metres away but closing fast. Doug only had time for a single, crouched cast. Fortunately it was a good one, landing his stick caddis, which hung barely a foot beneath the indicator, just over the black pipe and right on line with the oncoming trout. With a couple of metres to go, Doug gave the fly the tiniest twitch. The reaction from the trout was immediate as it accelerated over to the fly … and stopped. I strained to see through the washed-out surface while watching the indicator at the same time. The little piece of white wool didn't so much as shudder, but I imagined I saw the trout's head twitch deliberately. 'Strike!' I yelled. Doug, bless him, lifted the rod immediately and the trout was on. You can imagine the fight as a 9-pound brown felt the hook in ankle-deep water. There were several extremely tense minutes, including a period when the trout somehow swam under the pipe and straight towards Doug, thereby causing the line to transcribe an ominous hairpin shape. But Doug kept his cool and finally I was able to slide the net under the largest trout he'd ever landed.

There was celebration and several photographs before the trout swam off to hopefully grow a few pounds heavier. It was a relatively young fish with a small head on its round, greenish-gold body, and we speculated that next time the trout was caught, it would probably have grown beyond the magic 10-pound mark. We also replayed the whole event. Too often big trout stories don't have a happy ending and it was a rare luxury to talk about what went right, rather than conducting a more morose examination of where things failed. Hindsight vindicated a number of decisions: counting on the trout to return on its beat, using a stick caddis, suspending the fly off the bottom (just) by using an indicator. 'But the thing I still can't believe was your call to strike,' said Doug, 'when the indicator never moved.' He shook his head and added, 'I just wouldn't have lifted the rod at all — I couldn't see the fish and wouldn't have dared.'

That episode shows just how difficult it can be to detect wet-fly takes. Even with a tight line between indicator and the fly only a handspan away, if the trout stops to eat, or comes slowly straight at the angler at the moment it eats, there simply isn't a way for the line or any other tool to signal a take. To compound the problem, as soon as the fish tastes and smells a mistake or feels any unusual resistance, it will spit out the fly and the chance is gone. Would Doug's trout have hung on long enough to move the indicator, and would he then have been able to respond quickly enough to set the hook? It's possible but unlikely. I'm sure many of the trout we miss while indicator fishing are behaving just like Doug's, and by the time we see the indicator move, the trout is actually trying to eject the fly.

The overall lesson is, back your judgement. If you're nymphing a river or sight fishing a lake with a wet fly and you think the trout has eaten your fly, despite no evidence from your tackle: lift. You'll get it wrong occasionally, but right more often. The rule is simple: if in doubt, strike. Follow that and you'll catch many more trout than if you're always waiting for some sort of hard confirmation.

By way of contrast, bait fishers have the luxury of an offering that not only looks good but tastes good too. This means they can afford to wait until it's certain the fish has taken before lifting the rod. However, this strategy won't work on a fraud that fails the taste test: a trout won't keep chewing on a fly that doesn't taste right, and it won't spit out a fly and then come back for seconds in case it was wrong the first time. The wet-fly strike is now or never; do or die. Forgive me if I'm labouring the point, but there is no second chance — at least not with that particular fish.

On many occasions, like when the light is poor, the water is broken or discoloured, or the fly is being fished very deep, there is no option but to rely on the movement of the indicator. But once again, if in doubt ... And don't assume anything spectacular will happen to the indicator when a trout eats your fly. Rather than dive for the bottom as if snagged on a speeding shark, indicators will often merely quiver, hesitate or slowly submerge in response to a take. This applies on lake or stream.

The same logic regarding the potential subtlety of the take and a committed, decisive response from the angler applies to all other forms of wet-fly fishing. When *retrieving* wet flies, for example, many flyfishers remain fixed to the mistaken belief that, because they're pulling the fly towards them on a reasonably tight line, they'll feel the take. *Au contraire* — and I speak from experience. It was some years before I realised that *lots* of trout eat retrieved flies without being felt through the line. Instead you must watch the fly line; trout can move the line a surprising amount before you feel them, if at all.

It was an English competition angler (thanks Martin!) who finally convinced me that anyone retrieving a wet fly — fast or slow — should keep an eagle eye on the normally concave bridge of fly line between the rod tip and the water. Any lifting or straightening of this bridge should be met with a strike. Once you know what to look for, it's quite extraordinary to discover how often fish take your retrieved wet fly without you feeling the take. Some days the difference is sobering. On one occasion when the trout were being especially subtle, I dedicated myself to watching a client's line and calling the strike on movement alone. After about half-a-dozen 'bridge lifts' he got the hang of it. After 21 takes without a single one being felt before striking, he didn't know whether to be elated or dejected. 'To think how many trout I've missed over the years and never known it,' he sighed.

'Well, at least you found out now,' I comforted, knowing just how it felt when I received the same revelation, 'and not in another twenty years.'

PLAYING TROUT

THE OTHER DAY I was guiding a gentleman, whom I shall thinly disguise with the name Pierre, when he hooked a very large, fit trout. As this rainbow went streaking out into the lake and Pierre's reel spun like a wheel on an out-of-control billy cart, I asked, 'How much backing have you got?'

My intention, of course, was to establish if he had dangerously little — say, 50 metres — or enough, like 100 metres or more. 'Err, none,' replied Pierre, looking both sheepish and stricken at once. Sure enough, within a heartbeat or two of me asking the question, I observed alloy appearing beneath the last few coils of his fly line. There was no choice but to advise Pierre to clamp the line against the cork. For a fleeting moment, the bend in the rod absorbed the impact of this manoeuvre, and then the inevitable happened. The tippet broke and the biggest trout Pierre will quite likely ever hook was gone. If there was any silver lining to this sorry incident it was that he didn't lose $120 worth of fly line as well.

A few seconds of silence followed. Then, when I felt I was able to talk again without sounding like Gordon Ramsay, I asked Pierre why he had no backing. 'Well, on the streams I usually fish, the trout are mostly small, so I figured I'd never need backing,' he responded, in a tone that suggested he already accepted the shortcomings of this logic. That is, you don't need backing ... until you really, really need backing. A bit like a seat belt.

Backing is one of the essential components for a happy outcome when you hook a big trout. And that's what this chapter is really about: successfully landing big fish. Playing trout is mostly a non-event if they are small. Small trout are still great fun to catch, of course; and there are many parts of the process that can be as challenging as any when fishing to ... well, let's call them 'less big' trout. However, unless you are fishing at the extreme end of light tippet, trout under a pound or so are only likely to escape if the hook pulls out.

The reverse is true with larger trout — I'll generalise here and say trout over 3 pounds. Assuming 'regular' tippets, say in the 4 to 8-pound range, such fish will mostly be capable of breaking the line if you make a mistake. Obviously, the bigger the trout in relation to the tippet, the smaller the mistake needs to be. The other variable is environment. Trout in swift rivers are at an advantage, so too are fish that have easy access to line-snagging or breaking structure like thick weed, sticks or big rocks.

The fish-playing equation begins with sensible tippet. Tippet deserves its own chapter, which is coming up, but for now I will simply define 'sensible tippet' as no weaker than necessary. Next comes drag setting. I'm sure your reel has an adjustable drag — not owning a reel with a decent drag is a bit like not having backing. When setting the drag, do so while hooking the fly on something well beyond the tip, then pull to see if the resistance feels right. Simply testing drag by pulling line straight off the reel doesn't allow for the added resistance of the line travelling over several runners on a bent rod.

If I seem to be devoting a lot of ink to the whole subject of successfully landing big fish, it may partly be because, as a guide, I too often see the disappointment of big fish lost. Some of these trout are lost through what might be termed circumstances beyond our control — mostly fish that find cover despite rods being bent and tippets stretched to the limit. Such losses can be accepted with good grace, and although you may feel a tinge of sadness, you at least have the consolation when you replay things in your mind that there was nothing you could have done to avoid the outcome. *C'est la vie.*

It's all the other large fish gone that haunt me a little, so here are some things you can do to help limit the break-offs. First, keep your rod at right angles to the line *at all times.* Pointing the rod at the fish may work in the salt with very heavy tippets, but when trout fishing, it is exactly how you would break the line if you hooked an unwanted species or a snag. A bent rod is not a saviour on its own, but it is a shock absorber, a way to buy a few seconds of reaction time, or to deny a big trout that sudden jolt it needs to easily snap the tippet. The single most common way I see trout broken off is when the angler holds on to the line a moment too long and their rod is pulled down before they know it. There follows a nasty collision between a trout that has momentum and a direct line that has no give.

Often, an angler broken off this way is genuinely unaware of what went wrong. Or else they are aware but thought they'd got away with it. 'But I only dropped the rod for a moment,' is a common protest, as if the fishing gods might retrospectively reattach the trout in sympathy.

To the second point: let the trout run. Once a trout is hooked, we all have an almost primal urge to pull it to the bank as quickly as possible. Having gone to all that trouble to hook the fish in the first place, we want to rush to the next victorious step of having actually caught it. I often tell others (and remind myself) that this is exactly what a big trout would hope we'd do — assuming big trout could think, which they can't. An angler in a hurry to land a large fish is an angler on a tightrope. Tippets are constantly near breaking point; little mistakes are amplified.

On the other hand, the best fish-players I know maintain a cool, unrushed appearance — at least on the outside! The trout is often allowed to run great distances, before being carefully cranked back in, then permitted to run again if need be. This tactic is not about letting the trout do whatever it likes; there is considerable control in terms of steering the fish in the right direction and applying pressure at the right moment and in the right way. For example, clever anglers will encourage the trout to swim into the current and will whenever possible apply pressure in the opposite direction to where the trout's head is pointing.

At some point, decided as much by the trout and circumstances as by the angler, the fish will finally be within netting range. This is a good time to diverge for a bit and talk about landing nets. Like backing, you don't really *need* a net until the moment arrives when your present and future fishing happiness depends on having one. Now granted, there are times when a net is no better option for landing a good trout than, say, beaching it on a gently sloping edge or gravel bank. But when you're standing 50 metres out in the lake and you hook a monster, or in the middle of a fast river strewn with boulders like medicine balls, you either need a net or a miracle.

'But what about those Jim Allen films?' I hear someone ask. 'He's standing in waist-deep water and lifting out huge trout by hand — not a net in sight!' Two things about that. First, Jim is hardly a valid sample of the typical angler. He has had so much practice landing big trout that he could probably grab them with his teeth if he wanted to. Second, when you've landed as many seriously big trout as Jim has, you can, unlike most of us, afford to lose a few.

I trust, then, that we can take it as a given that you should carry a landing net anywhere there's even a remote chance of hooking a trout you don't want to lose. The next question is, 'Which net?' The most important thing to acknowledge here is that as attractive as some landing nets are, they are first and foremost a tool not an ornament. No matter how lovingly carved the walnut handle, how finely crafted the silver inlay, a landing net is useless — no, worse than useless — if it's not big enough to easily accommodate the largest trout you might ever encounter. A landing net that's about the right size for removing your child's dead goldfish from its bowl, or straining tea, should never be allowed anywhere near good trout water. I live in hope that the day will come when a fisheries inspector can measure a landing net, find it less than 50 centimetres in diameter and less than 60 centimetres deep, and send the offending angler back to the car for a good long think about what the heck they thought they were doing. On the other hand, anyone found carrying a net big enough to cope with a Lake Awoonga barra, would be congratulated and awarded a free fishing licence for a year.

As for folding nets, two brief points. If they require any thought at all to assemble while you're locked in battle with a trophy, then we have a problem, don't we? We also have a problem if the net decides on its own when to fold up again. My good friend John had a folding net that worked perfectly until one day, on the King River, he skilfully netted a 5-pounder, only to find out that the frame clips detached under a load of more than 4.5 pounds. While I don't approve of littering, I can understand why John's net now lies in a hundred pieces somewhere on the river's forested bank.

Carry a functional net with you at all times and you are two-thirds of the way towards a happy outcome in the event you fight a large trout to within net range. However, there remains the matter of using the net correctly. A potent truth to remember is that the slowest trout is faster than the quickest human. In other words, no matter how speedy your swipe at a moving trout, the fish will be speedier. I've alluded to the consequences of the net swipe in previous writings, none of them pretty. These include slicing through the tippet, catching the hook on the outside of the mesh, and tossing the fish to certain freedom like a bad chef attempting to flip an omelette.

The trick is to bring the trout to the net, not the other way around. Towards the end of a long struggle, it is hard to resist the temptation to hurry things up, but it is much safer to lead the fish to the net, head first. When you reach this point, the net can be gracefully slid around the trout. If you have the right net in terms of size and structural integrity (and of course you now do) then this is the moment of relief, certainty and celebration. Aren't you glad you didn't leave the net in the car?

TIPPET

A LONG-STANDING FISHING friend of mine, whom we shall call Jagger, recently returned from his first trip to Westland in the South Island of New Zealand. Having fished that area a bit, my advice was sought and Jagger's journey was preceded by many phone calls and chats at my kitchen table. Maps were pulled out, fly boxes examined, important gear ticked off a list. And that's where I partly blame myself. Through oversight or misplaced confidence in Jagger's knowledge (he's fished other parts of New Zealand before, including landing the best fish either of us has caught there), I didn't mention tippet.

Upon his return, Jagger's report was upbeat in most respects — pretty good weather, fish visible and taking the fly well, clear water ... However, there was one major blight on the trip: he didn't land a single big fish. Every one broke him off. With sinking heart I asked Jagger what tippet he'd used? 'Oh, 6-pound Weakstream,' he replied, as if wondering what that had to do with anything.

'Weakstream!' I hissed, in the same tone Blackadder reserves for Baldrick and Seinfeld saves for Newman. So that was it. Unless a large trout ate his fly and immediately died, poor Jagger never stood a chance.

For something so critical to trout fishing success, the importance of tippet is extraordinarily underrated by most flyfishers. Granted, if you're fishing for trout no bigger than the span of your outstretched hand, tippet — like nets, backing and playing fish — is a topic you can avoid without much fish-catching penalty. However, for any other situation a thorough understanding of the whole tippet thing is essential to avoid unnecessary heartache, a big bill in flies, and, dare I say it, unhappy guides. And by the way, if you want to test the value guides place on tippet, you need only casually but obviously start tying on some of your own tippet. A good guide will be on to you as if you're a toddler playing with matches.

The main purpose of tippet is to present flies in a way that's acceptable to the trout, while at the same time providing a link between you and the fish strong enough to provide a reasonable chance of landing it. There is no reliable (I said *reliable*) formula to help determine what tippet should be used with a given fly in a given situation. However, there are some points worth considering when you choose your tippet. Firstly, and fundamentally, in daylight trout can nearly always see the tippet and reducing its diameter by a few microns isn't going to make it suddenly disappear like a magician's trick. So why bother using finer tippet at all?

Well, trout may always be able to see the tippet but it's whether they associate it with the fly that matters. Fortunately, trout aren't bright enough to analyse things too comprehensively, which is why they will eat a fly despite a fairly incongruous hook sticking out the bottom. But there is a limit to what's acceptable, and trout will draw the line (sorry!) at tippet that looks like a broom handle sticking out of a bug's head. This is one reason we can't fish 10-pound (about .009-inch) tippet with a size 18 dry fly, even though, at the same place at the same moment, it's quite acceptable to use it with a size 6 Assassin.

Closely related to this point is the issue of fly behaviour. Flies tied to tippet that's relatively fine in relation to their size swim or float more naturally. An average-sized dun pattern fished on .007-inch tippet will bob on the wavelets pretty much as a natural would, whereas one tied to a piece of leader butt might as well be stuck on a strand of fencing wire. Needless to say, the fluidity of movement in flies retrieved or drifted beneath the surface is likewise enhanced by fine tippet, or reduced by tippet that's too thick. And speaking of below the surface, fine tippet sinks more easily than thick, and so is better suited to situations where you need your flies down deep, and you want them there fairly quickly.

It might superficially be assumed then that, leaving aside landing big trout, finer always equals better. However, it's far from that simple. To begin with, all but the most aerodynamic flies will twist tippet if it's too fine in relation to fly size. Woolly Buggers or large hackled dry flies and the like are notorious for this and will present as if attached to a coiled spring unless reasonably thick tippet is used. Speaking of dries, fishing large dries like a Black Muddler at night actually benefits from thicker tippet that helps to keep the fly on top where you want it (not to mention giving you a much needed edge when you hook a monster).

Which brings us back to the best reason not to use fine tippet: it is simply more likely to break. While tippet diameter and breaking strain is not an entirely tidy relationship (more on this shortly) the trend is there. Anyway, at the risk of approaching the point from the negative, I continually see the same three tippet problems among my flyfishing colleagues and clients:

- tippet is chosen that's too weak for a given fishing situation,
- all brands are wrongly regarded as equal and interchangeable,
- the fact that tippet can age and deteriorate is overlooked.

To the first point: I'd rather land fish than have them break me off. However, I fish with lots of people who seem to be on a quest, wittingly or not, to see just how big a trout they can land on cobweb — until it inevitably breaks. At this point they look equal parts distraught and as if they've awoken from an evil spell. My own tippet mantra is simple: fish as heavy as you can get away with.

To explore this tack a little further, I must grudgingly touch on the subject of the X system. My stock-standard tippet choice is .008 inch, or 3X. In the brands I prefer, this equates to an honest 7 to 8-pound breaking strain. I will use .009 inch (2X) for big wets or dries if I can get away with it. If small flies (say size 14 to 18) demand it, I will take a deep breath and change to .007 inch (4X) tippet, which is around 6-pound breaking strain. Notice the backward X system? Silly isn't it, and how much easier a flyfishing instructor's life would be if our fly forefathers had just decided to remove the zeros: size 9 tippet (.009 inch), size 8, 7, etc. Most people would immediately grasp that the descending number meant finer, weaker tippet. But we're stuck with the xxxx X system, so all I can do is suggest you look at the diameter and breaking strain, not the X, when choosing tippet.

Which brings me to brand. Few categories of flyfishing equipment vary as starkly in performance as different brands of tippet. Over many years of fishing to big trout and guiding others on to them, I've narrowed down a few brands that I trust. These elite few will break eventually, but all have avoided the 'What the #$@!?' bust-offs that blight lesser brands. I'm not going to list the best; for a start, I would inevitably overlook very good brands I haven't tried yet, which is unfair. But when you go to buy tippet, recognise the vast differences in quality and seek the advice of a trusted guide, tackle rat or fishing mate, with the proviso that they have caught lots of big fish. Your typical twig fisher may be a gifted angler, but they probably can't speak with authority about strong tippet.

In short, all tippet brands are likely to break around their stated breaking strain when pressure is applied directly off the spool in the shop. But in practical terms, things like knot strength, abrasion resistance and shock absorption are at least as important when playing real fish in real situations

Lastly, tippet corrupted by age, sun or extreme heat can't be trusted. Period. Give it a sad wave goodbye if you wish but then pass it to the rubbish bin or a fishing acquaintance you don't particularly like — maybe an advocate of the X system perhaps?

THE TRIP

I'M OFF TO the Snowy Mountains today, being the second day of summer. It's been a busy few months with guiding, writing and editing and, as with many springs where trout fishing opportunities seem to multiply at an exponential rate, I've done less fishing — as in, fishing myself — than I'd like. I never made it to Lake Eildon for what might have been sublime, once-in-twenty-year floodwater feeder fishing. Nor have I managed to pick a gap in the floods to fish the superb Kossie dun hatches I hear are occurring on the Kiewa. Even the high-water fishing on the south-west Victorian rivers has eluded me this spring, and I had to knock back Felix's offer to join him for some early season fishing out of his lodge — that really hurt. Okay, I had a cracking week in Tasmania, my best fishing yet in the Grampians and a couple of great days at Purrumbete and Bullen Merri, but you know what I mean.

So today is an exciting day. Jane will drive me to the airport with my little boys (the planes landing and taking off, not to mention all the coin-controlled train and fire-engine rides, make this quite an outing for them). I will begin missing them and Jane within about an hour of taking off, but I'll be away for less than a week so I will cope. Steve will meet me at the other end in Canberra — he's gradually spending more time there than at his place in Sydney — then we'll embark on the $1\frac{1}{2}$-hour drive to the Snowy Mountains themselves.

This isn't an impromptu trip. Steve invited me months ago; neither of us have such empty schedules that we can coordinate five days fishing together with a week's notice. But while I dislike my life being planned too far in advance, in this case I've become progressively more grateful for this particular highlighted period. Without it I can see those days would have easily fallen to pre-Christmas parties, work and the other little things that can slowly eat away at fishing chances while you barely notice.

With any trip locked in months ahead, it pays to build in some flexibility and Steve and I have. The destination marked on the calendar on the kitchen wall is simply 'The Snowy Mountains', which equates to roughly 10,000 square kilometres of forest, mountains, gorges, plateaus and farmland. The area also contains who knows how many thousand kilometres of trout stream and thousands of hectares of trout lakes. So this gives us options: a handy ingredient on any successful fishing trip, and downright essential for one planned before lake or stream conditions can possibly be predicted.

Our care in not being too prescriptive about an itinerary has paid off. The area has just experienced one of the wettest springs in decades and the usual early summer patterns have been skewed. We had hoped to fish the streams at least some of the time, but that is now looking unlikely. I've been checking the daily rainfall totals on the Bureau of Meteorology site as departure date looms and the catchment gauges at places like Cabramurra and Perisher have had nearly 100 millimetres just this week. That's on the back of months of rain and snow. Even Cooma, normally located in a rain-shadow, has been wet.

Usually I prefer to reach my own conclusions when assessing the state of the fishing before a trip. I've found over the decades that regular fishing reports — both formal and informal — tend to be pretty much useless. A combination of inexperienced anglers talking to anyone who'll listen and experienced anglers keeping quiet about the best of the fishing leads to reports that are basically worthless. My rule of thumb for fishing reports is to ignore them unless I know and respect the angler offering them.

In the case of the Snowys, the rare luxury of a couple of tackle shops with reputable reporters, plus two or three mates who regularly fish there, means I make an exception here and I take the reports I've been receiving seriously. By all accounts the rivers are indeed far too high. Now that isn't to say we couldn't fish the backwaters and edges and possibly catch some of the very nice trout which have undoubtedly stayed up from the lakes with all that big water. However, it is going to be hard to take restricted river fishing over lake fishing conditions that might just be perfect. Lake Eucumbene is rising slowly over ground that was inundated last year but only briefly. (I know this by comparing lake height graphs from last year and this year on the Snowy Hydro website; I also know because my local contact Chris was kind enough to tell me and he fished there last Friday!) This means the lake is submerging ground with some vegetation and some terrestrial life, but not so much as to create a glut. And the shores will be clean and easy to fish.

The computer models and the forecasts all agree it will be overcast, not too hot, not too cold and not too windy. Perfect for lakes, and to be fair, pretty good for rivers too should we want a change of scenery. Lake Tantangara could be interesting. The graphs show it will be at a fourteen-year high and pushing right back into the tussocks and scrub. Many shores will be too messy to fish, but the lake teems with trout and they will be better than average size with all that flooded ground. Lake Jindabyne is in a similar situation, although Trevor, who lives beside the lake, tells me the 'non-messy' shores are increasingly limited, and the lake will be rising fast — too fast to really concentrate the trout in the extreme shallows. I feel disappointed that I may miss out on fishing a favourite lake under decade-high conditions; I know there will be very big trout swimming there. But as I said earlier in this book, it's important to cold-bloodedly assess the facts when it comes to conditions and likely trout behaviour. Wanting or hoping things will be a certain way doesn't really work; well, not with nature anyway. Nature does what it does, and a good flyfisher fits in.

A successful trip obviously requires the right gear. Our accommodation options wherever we end up will include a roof, four walls, running water and electricity. Camping in the rain is something to be avoided, so I don't need to worry about the extensive camping checklist.

Fishing in the rain is another matter. This week we are likely to see a lot of it, so I'm packing accordingly. All the good computer models — GFS, UKMET, EC and ACCESS (accessible these days from any computer) — agree that rain will be an issue but not the cold. The Bureau of Meteorology forecast for the Snowy Mountains region concurs. So thermal underwear, gloves and balaclava can be left behind. I will, however, be taking full-length breathable waders and my brilliant breathable shell jacket which I picked up last year at a half-price sale. Once again I will avoid naming brands, but let me assure you that, of the many breathable jacket materials that promise to keep you dry, very few do. Showerproof is not enough for a serious angler; a good jacket is one that will keep you dry in a four-hour deluge. Ask anyone who spends lots of time in the rain for advice on brands, not a shop assistant.

Some people treat rain as if it's some evil chemical falling out of the sky rather than the basis of all life. But if you dress for it, you can have some fine fishing in the rain and I for one will not be travelling 700 kilometres to read cheap service station novels or yesterday's newspaper — about the extent of the indoor entertainment where we're going.

While I think of it, a wide-brim hat and sunscreen will still be essential when the sun comes out, which it's bound to do for a few hours. The sun is killer strength at this time of year, and besides, a broad brim will help to keep the rain off my face at other times. Which reminds me, I should pack sun gloves too. And with the sun or any warmth will come swarms of flies and mossies, so I'm putting some repellant in my vest as we speak. I noticed my New South Wales fishing licence when I did that and it's current.

For fishing gear, 'rod-reel-vest-waders' (plus in this case my separate soft rubber-soled wading boots) is a reliable mantra. I won't add tungsten boot studs to the list because, as I've already mentioned, I doubt we'll do too much river fishing, and if we do, I don't plan on wading far into water that would be dangerous to kayak. My polaroids (yellowish-amber tint) are already in my vest. I will take my landing net too despite the fact it will probably (should that be hopefully?) be wet and smelly when I repack it for the trip home.

A big trip like this one is a good time to replace my fly line, which is becoming increasingly cracked and sticky after eighteen months of loyal service. To the line I will add a new 9-foot mono leader — 2X of course. I will wait until I get to the water tomorrow before adding tippet, but I expect it will be about 3 feet of 3X (8-pound) high-quality fluorocarbon. If there are flying ants or termites on the lake — a fair chance in the forecast thundery weather — I may go down to 4X for the small imitative dries that will be essential. An evening midge hatch will also be a good chance at this time of year, in which case the 4X will be on for sure. However, watch me cut it off and go straight back to the 2X leader tip if we get a fine night and the mudeyes migrate.

It goes without saying that on a trip of more than a few hours you bring a spare rod in case of breakage, and I'll be taking my trusty six-piece which can fit snuggly in my day bag wherever we travel over the next few days. A 5-weight, it's lighter than my 7-weight lake rod which, under the circumstances, I see as the main rod for this trip; however, if we do manage to find some stream fishing it will be perfect for the job.

Finally, I'll be taking the camera and a waterproof bag so I can carry it everywhere in the rain without worry. This trip is a fishing holiday but a fishing writer is never entirely off duty, and besides, if Steve or I catch a monster, it would be nice to have a record, story or not. I will take my diary, which is to be completed regardless.

I think that's about it. I could carry a spare pair of polaroids; however, Steve usually carries an extra pair which should be sufficient back-up for both of us. The fly supply is pretty good. You can't plan for every eventuality but I have checked which fly boxes are in my vest and which are out. I think I've got the likely events covered, even a few not-so-likely ones.

Wallet, phone, ticket ... so that's it, I'm off. Wish me luck.

A WORD ON MEASUREMENTS

IN MY PREVIOUS book, *Fishing Season*, my editor made the perfectly reasonable request that I address the inconsistency of using both imperial and metric measurements. Two years on and things haven't got any better, so I'd better repeat my reasoning ...

Most Australian and New Zealand flyfishers, including flyfishing writers, swap cheerfully (if at times confusingly) from imperial measurements to metric and back again. The sympathetic explanation relates to the dominance of American, or outsourced American, product across much of the global flyfishing market. Rods and fly lines are frequently labelled in feet and inches, tippet breaking strains are often listed in pounds, and so on. The issue is not helped by the reluctance of Britain, another English-speaking force in flyfishing, to adopt the metric system.

So, even antipodean flyfishers born after the 1970s soon develop some understanding of imperial measurements when buying gear, or when consulting international texts and websites. David, the youngest of the guides I work with and barely out of his teens, still tells me of the 6-pounder his client just caught, not the 2.7 kilogram fish.

Which brings me to a second explanation for the partial failure of metrification in flyfishing: fish, especially trout, just sound bigger when described in pounds. Moreover, of the unofficial 'benchmark' weights when flyfishing for trout — 1 pound (450 grams), 2 pounds (roughly 1 kilogram), and 10 pounds (4.5 kilograms) — only the middle one doesn't sound ridiculous in metric. The exception occurs when your fish is so large that you can describe it in kilos and it still sounds big.

Meanwhile, distances beyond casting range (and sometimes within) are happily described in metric. For Australian and New Zealand flyfishers, the distance to a lake is most meaningfully described in kilometres, while the bay where the fish are rising is likely to be at least a 400-metre walk.

Some useful flyfishing conversions

1 inch = 2.54 centimetres
1 foot = 30.4 centimetres
1 yard = 0.94 metres (yards and metres are roughly interchangeable)
1 pound = 454 grams
1 kilogram = 2.2 pounds

ACKNOWLEDGEMENTS

My thanks to all my fishing companions for their thoughts and advice over the years. Time and repetition make it difficult to attribute credit to everyone who deserves it, so I hope it's enough to say I'm very lucky to have spent time with fisheries scientists and long-time anglers who've been able to prod my own theories and observations and, of course, offer their own.

INDEX